WHERE SHADOWS FALL

WHERE SHADOWS FALL

DANNY NIÑAL

Contents

Dedication	v
PROLOGUE	1
1 A City in Distress	4
2 Shadows in the Alleyways	7
3 Unraveling the Threads of Deceit	11
4 Shadows and Suspects	16
5 A Legacy of Courage	18
6 A Shared Burden – Unveiling the Past	21
7 Web of Deceit – Unraveling the Identity Theft	24
8 The Street's Whisper – A Network Unfolds	27
9 Shadows of Conspiracy – A Gathering Storm	32
10 The Banker's Gambit – A Web of Deceit	36
11 The Casino King - High Stakes and High Risks	39
12 The Shadow of David	43
13 Fractured Trust	45
14 Shadows of Betrayal	49
15 The Call of Brotherhood	53
16 Crumbling Control	55
17 Unveiling Mr. K – The Past	58
18 Shifting Sands	62

19	Operation Medusa	65
20	A Frantic Meeting	68
21	Operation Medusa - Endgame	71
22	A House Divided	74
23	The Price of Rescue	77
24	Desperate Measures	79
25	Extraction	81
26	Sunsets and Shadows	84
27	New Dawn	86
	List of Characters	88
	THE PARK CHRONICLES	89
	I DIED THEREFORE I AM by Danny Niñal	90
	WHAT IS PLEASURE WITHOUT PAIN	97
	APPEARANCES	104
	LOVE: A MONKEY'S BUSINESS	113
	THE SEARCH	122

About the Author   132

This is dedicated to my only daughter, Danielle Angelika Niñal.

Copyright @ 2025 by Danny Niñal
Published in Australia by: BMN Publishing
Cover and Interior Design by: Danny Niñal
Photo by: Pete Galula

All rights reserve. No part of this book may be reproduced by any mechanical, photographic, or electronic process or in the form of a phonographic recording; nor may it be stored in a retrieval system, transmitted, or otherwise be copied for public or private use – other than for "fair use" as brief quotation embodied in articles and reviews – without prior written permission of the publisher.

The Author/Publisher has strived to be as accurate and complete as possible in the creation of this book, notwithstanding the fact that he does not warrant or represent at any time that the contents within are accurate due to the rapidly changing nature of the Internet.

This is a work of fiction. Names, characters, businesses, places, events, locales, and incidents are either the products of the author's imagination or used in a fictitious manner. Any resemblance to actual persons, living or dead, or actual events is purely coincidental.

Cataloguing-in-Publication Data is on file at the National Library of Australia.

ISBM 978-1-7637990-1-1

Printed in Australia by Lightning Source Printing Company

Copyright @ 2024
BMN Publishing.
All Rights Reserved

PROLOGUE

Prologue: Dust and Echoes

The pre-dawn chill clung to the air at base camp, a stark contrast to the scorching heat that awaited them. Ysabel checked her gear, her movements precise and efficient, a practiced routine honed by years of experience. Liam approached, his eyes crinkling at the corners as he smiled. He held out a small, worn, leather-bound book—A Copy of Poetry.

"For you," he said, his voice low and tender. "Something to keep you company on the long nights."

Ysabel took the book, her fingers brushing his. A warmth spread through her, a feeling that transcended the harsh reality of their surroundings. They stood for a moment, and the silence filled only with the distant hum of generators and the rustle of the wind.

"After this," Liam said, his gaze intense, "we're getting married."

Ysabel's breath caught in her throat. The words hung in the air, a promise whispered against the backdrop of impending danger. She nodded, a tear tracing a path down her cheek. "Yes," she replied, her voice thick with emotion. "After this."

They embraced a brief, silent moment of intimacy, a fragile bubble of love in a world of harsh realities. Then, the harsh reality of their mission intruded.

The Afghan sun beat down, a merciless hammer forging the parched earth into a shimmering mirage. Dust devils danced across the barren landscape, swirling like malevolent spirits. The air hung heavy, thick with the scent of sun-baked earth and the metallic tang of fear. Liam's hand brushed hers, a fleeting touch that spoke volumes—a silent promise, a shared understanding in the face of impending danger. Their mission: a rescue operation deep within enemy territory.

The air crackled with unspoken tension, a palpable energy that vibrated between them and the rest of the team.

A woman walked along the roadside, her gait oddly stiff, her eyes darting nervously. Ysabel's gaze locked with hers for a heartbeat—a flicker of something unnatural, a subtle tremor in her hand, the way she clutched her bag too tightly. *Improvised explosive device,* Ysabel's mind screamed. *She's a trigger.* The thought was instantaneous, intuitive, a cold certainty that settled deep in her gut. Without hesitation, she barked a command, her voice cutting through the tense silence: "Team, scramble! Now!"

The ambush erupted—a storm of gunfire and chaos that tore through the fragile peace. The world exploded in a cacophony: the sharp crack of gunfire, the guttural shouts of the enemy, the screams of her men. Dust and debris rained down, obscuring vision and turning the familiar landscape into a nightmarish battlefield. Ysabel's quick thinking had given half her team a crucial head start, allowing them to take cover and return fire, but it wasn't enough to prevent the ambush entirely. A figure emerged from the swirling dust, a grenade launcher trained on their armored personnel vehicle (APV). Ysabel reacted instantly, her weapon rising as if an extension of her own body, her focus unwavering. She squeezed the trigger, the shot echoing—a sharp, precise crack—and the enemy soldier crumpled, the grenade launcher clattering to the ground. The potential catastrophe averted, for now.

But the ambush raged on. The enemy, a swarm of shadowy figures, closed in, their weapons spitting death. Ysabel fought, a whirlwind of controlled fury. Her training took over, her movements precise and deadly. She took down several of them, her shots finding their marks with chilling accuracy. But the enemy was relentless, their numbers overwhelming. One by one, her team fell, their screams swallowed by the roar of battle.

Liam, caught in the open, stumbled, a crimson stain blooming across his chest. He cried out, his voice lost in the cacophony of war. Ysabel scrambled to him, pushing through the hail of bullets, her heart pounding in her chest. She reached him, her fingers frantic against the wound, trying to stem the flow of blood. His eyes, wide and filled with pain, met hers. "Ysabel..." he whispered, his voice barely audible above the chaos. She held him, his body trembling, his life ebbing away in her arms. The weight of his death settled upon her like a shroud, the crushing weight of her failure.

Then, the roar of helicopters, the staccato bursts of air support fire, silencing the enemy. The dust settled, leaving behind a landscape of death and the bitter taste of survival. She held him, his life fading, his eyes mirroring her own grief, the weight of his loss settling upon her like a shroud. His last breath hitched a silent farewell. His eyes, wide and filled with pain, met hers one last time before closing forever. The dog tag, cold and metallic against her palm, a constant, chilling reminder of her survival and his loss.

1

A City in Distress

The aroma of freshly brewed coffee and sizzling pancakes hung heavy in the crisp morning air, a comforting blanket against the chill that clung to the city streets. "Breakfast of Champions," a twice-weekly charity event, was in full swing. Laughter and cheerful chatter filled the air, a vibrant counterpoint to the usual grimness of the abandoned lot where it took place. Volunteers bustled about, their smiles as warm as the steaming mugs they handed out. Ysabel, the city's mayor, moved effortlessly through the crowd, her presence a beacon of hope in this often-forgotten corner of the city.

Ysabel was a familiar sight, tall and breathtaking even in her practical attire. Her sharp eyes usually focused on city budgets and political maneuvering, scanned the faces of the homeless people with genuine warmth. They knew her by name, some even calling her "Ysabel," a testament to her authentic connection with this often-ignored segment of the city's demographics. She was their champion, a symbol of hope in a town that often forgot them.

Beside her, Detective Inspector Ethan Cole, a man whose quiet strength belied his easy smile, moved with a similar grace. Tall and good-looking, with a hint of weariness etched around his eyes, he possessed a quiet intensity that spoke of years spent navigating the city's underbelly. He was a widower, his grief a quiet weight he carried with dignity. His dedication to helping the homeless was as unwavering as his commitment to justice.

The usual joyous chatter was punctuated by bursts of laughter as people praised the mayor and her team of volunteers for their dedication. Their support wasn't just about food; it was about recognizing the humanity of those often overlooked. The homeless people, in turn, expressed their gratitude and unwavering support for both the mayor and the police, their voices a testament to the trust and respect they held for these two individuals who genuinely cared for their well-being.

Amidst the vibrant and joyous atmosphere, a woman sat alone, her eyes downcast, her shoulders slumped. She was a regular at the Breakfast of Champions, usually one of the most cheerful attendees, but today, she was different. Ysabel's keen eyes, honed by years of reading people, instantly picked up on the subtle shift in her demeanor. The woman's usual bright smile was absent, replaced by a haunted expression. Her hands trembled slightly as she held her coffee cup, a stark contrast to the lively energy around her.

Later, as the crowd thinned and the volunteers began packing up, Ysabel and Ethan found a quiet corner to discuss the situation.

"Seven missing in a week," Ethan said, his voice grave. "And all homeless. This isn't random."

"I agree," Ysabel replied, her tone serious. "The woman mentioned the warehouse. It's an abandoned building, but it's been a makeshift home for many homeless people for years. We need to check it out."

"I'll get a team together," Ethan said, his eyes already assessing the logistics. "We'll need to approach this carefully. We don't want to scare anyone off."

"And we need to be discreet," Ysabel added. "This could cause panic if it gets out to the public. We need to ensure the safety and well-being of the remaining homeless individuals."

Their conversation was brief but effective, a testament to their mutual understanding and commitment to solving the case. Their shared concern and determination were palpable, a silent promise to protect the vulnerable and bring the perpetrators to justice.

A silent exchange passed between Ysabel and Ethan. A single, knowing glance confirmed their shared understanding. This wasn't just another missing person's case; it was something far more sinister. The joyous atmosphere of the morning had been shattered, replaced by a heavy sense of foreboding. The investigation had begun. By the end of the day, the grim reality would be confirmed: seven people had vanished without a trace, and all of them had been homeless, their absence a chilling testament to a city in distress—seven people missing for at least seven days. The city's hidden wounds had begun to bleed.

2

Shadows in the Alleyways

The air in Ysabel's office was thick with tension, a stark contrast to the cheerful atmosphere of the Breakfast of Champions earlier that morning. On top of her table, beside the phone on the left side, lie prominently the small, worn, leather-bound book – a copy of poetry given by Liam. She touched it with her left hand. But that day was not the day to recall all types of memories, good or bad. Around the mahogany table sat her key staff: Councilman Javier Rodriguez, his face etched with worry; Chief of Staff Anya Sharma, her usually composed demeanor replaced by a furrow in her brow; and Police Liaison Officer David Chen, his usual jovial nature subdued. The city, usually vibrant and bustling, felt besieged.

"The disappearances," Ysabel began, calm but firm, "are escalating. Seven people were missing in a week. All homeless. This isn't just a coincidence."

Anya leaned forward, her fingers steepled beneath her chin. "The media is already picking up on it, Mayor. We need a strategy to address public concerns and fast. Panic could spread quickly."

Javier voiced his concerns, his gaze fixed on the city map spread across the table. "The homeless population is concentrated on the east side. The abandoned warehouse on Canal Street is a particular concern. It's been a makeshift home for many, but it's also known for attracting unsavory characters."

David, ever the pragmatist, chimed in. "We've increased patrols in the area, Mayor, but it's vast. We need more resources and more manpower. And we need to be careful not to cause undue alarm."

Ysabel nodded, her gaze sweeping across the faces of her staff. "We need to balance transparency with the need to maintain public order. We can't afford to fuel panic, but we also can't ignore the gravity of the situation. We need to find these people, and we need to do it quickly."

The discussion continued a complex interplay of concerns and strategies. They debated resource allocation, community outreach, and media relations. Ysabel listened intently, her sharp mind absorbing the information, and her leadership skills were evident in her ability to guide the conversation and synthesize the various perspectives. The weight of the city rested on her shoulders; the responsibility was heavy but not insurmountable. She was a leader and would find a way to navigate this crisis. But a deep-seated unease lingered a sense of foreboding that went beyond the immediate crisis.

Meanwhile, at police headquarters, Detective Inspector Ethan Cole stood before a whiteboard covered in photographs, names, and locations. His team—Sergeant Miller, a seasoned detective with a sharp eye for detail; Officer Diaz, a young but promising officer with a knack for technology; and forensic specialist Dr. Ramirez—surrounded him, their faces grim.

"The pattern is clear," Ethan stated, his voice low and measured. "All the missing individuals were last seen in the city's east side, primarily around the Canal Street warehouse. And they all seem connected to the city's homeless community."

Sergeant Miller tapped a photograph. "We've checked their backgrounds, Inspector. Most have minor offenses, nothing significant. But there's a common thread—they were all vulnerable, easy targets."

Officer Diaz chimed in, pointing to a map on the screen. "I've analyzed cell phone data, and there's a cluster of activity around the warehouse, then nothing. It's like they vanished into thin air."

Dr. Ramirez added, "The forensic evidence is minimal. There were no signs of struggle at any of their last known locations. It's almost as if they had been taken willingly."

Ethan nodded, his gaze fixed on the whiteboard. "This is a delicate situation. We need to proceed cautiously. A massive public search could scare off any potential witnesses or further endanger the remaining homeless population. We need a discreet approach, a surgical strike."

Ethan briskly addressed his team: "Keep me posted. Every detail counts. I need to brief the Mayor." He grabbed his jacket, his movements sharp and efficient. A quick text to Sergeant Miller confirmed their next steps. He strode purposefully towards the Mayor's office, the weight of the missing-persons case heavy on his shoulders.

"Inspector Cole," Trish Ropata, Ysabel's secretary, greeted him with a warm yet professional smile. Her calm demeanor starkly contrasted the somber atmosphere hanging over City Hall. "The Mayor is expecting you." She led him through the imposing double doors, her footsteps echoing softly on the polished floor.

Ysabel was already seated at her large desk. The city map spread before her. She looked up as Ethan entered, her expression serious but not unkind. "Coffee, Inspector?" she asked, her voice calm and reassuring.

Trish stepped forward, her movements precise and efficient. "The usual, sir?" she asked Ethan, her eyes already knowing the answer.

Ethan nodded, a small smile touching his lips. "Yes, please, Trish. Thank you." He appreciated the unspoken understanding and the subtle support amid the growing crisis. The unspoken acknowledgment of the gravity of the situation hung in the air, even in the simple exchange of a coffee order.

"You love poetry?" Ethan asked as he looked at the small, worn, leather-bound book – a Copy of Poetry.

"Oh. It's a gift from someone close to me," Ysabel replied. Ethan knew it was his queue to keep quiet.

Ysabel and Ethan were comparing notes. Their discussion focused on the potential connections between the missing persons and the city's other problems. The atmosphere was solemn, but collaboration and mutual respect were evident. They work well together, and their different approaches complement each other.

Suddenly, Ethan's phone rang. He glanced at the caller ID, a smile touching his lips.

"Excuse me," he says to Ysabel, answering the call. "Hey, baby...No, honey, I don't think that's a good idea tonight...No, I'm sorry, but I just don't think it's safe with everything going on...I love you, too. Yes, I'll see you later. Good night, sweetheart."

He hung up, and a sigh escaped his lips. "That was Lily," he explains to Ysabel, "asking if she could have a sleepover at her friend's house. I said no. With everything happening, I can't risk it."

Before Ysabel could respond, his phone rang again. Ethan answered immediately, his voice already laced with weariness.

"I already said no, baby," his tone firm but gentle. "Please...I love you."

There was a moment of stunned silence before Ethan realized the voice on the other end wasn't his daughter's. It was his boss, his voice tight with urgency.

"There were three bodies found in the river. They're believed to be among the missing persons reported earlier."

3

Unraveling the Threads of Deceit

Ysabel Ashworth and Detective Inspector Ethan Cole sat across from each other in Ysabel's office, the city map spread across the desk between them. The air hung heavy with the weight of the three bodies discovered on the cliffs. The coroner's report lay open, the stark details—time of death, cause of death, lack of struggle—offering little in the way of immediate answers. The grim facts seemed to mock their efforts.

Just as a frustrated silence threatened to settle, Ysabel's phone rang. It was the homeless woman from the Breakfast of Champions. Her voice, barely a whisper, sent a jolt through Ysabel.

"Mayor Ashworth," she gasped, "I...I heard something. One of the men—the one with the missing teeth—gave a huge amount of money to someone before he disappeared. They said it was enough to change their lives."

Ysabel's eyebrows shot up, her gaze locking with Ethan's. "How much?" she asked, her voice sharp with urgency.

"I don't know the exact amount," the woman replied, trembling. But they said it was a fortune—enough to buy a house, they said." The line went dead.

Ethan leaned forward, his gaze intense. "The suits...the cash...and now this. It's more than just a random act of violence." Though scattered, the puzzle pieces were beginning to form a disturbing pattern.

Ethan returned to Police Headquarters, the weight of the new information pressing down on him. His team was already gathered: Sergeant Miller, a seasoned detective with a cynical wit and an uncanny ability to read people; Officer Diaz, a young tech whiz with a restless energy and an almost supernatural ability to find information online; Dr. Ramirez, the forensic specialist, whose quiet intensity belied a sharp mind and an unwavering attention to detail; and Sarah Chen, the PR expert, whose calm demeanor masked a shrewd understanding of media manipulation.

Ethan briefed them on the call from the homeless woman, the tension palpable in the room. Sarah Chen, ever the pragmatist, immediately began drafting a press release, carefully balancing the need for transparency with the imperative to avoid widespread panic. Her fingers flew across the keyboard, crafting a informative and reassuring statement. She knew the delicate balance required to keep the public informed without fueling unnecessary fear.

Officer Diaz, meanwhile, his fingers dancing across his keyboard, delved into the digital world. His restless energy was channeled into a focused search for any online activity related to the victims. He was a master of his craft, able to sift through vast amounts of data with remarkable speed and efficiency. He wasn't just searching for information; he was hunting for clues, piecing together fragments of digital evidence to create a coherent picture.

His gaze fixed on the coroner's report, Dr. Ramirez meticulously reviewed the details, searching for any overlooked clues. His quiet intensity was infectious, a silent demand for precision and accuracy. He wasn't just a forensic specialist but a detective in his own right, able to extract meaning from seemingly insignificant details. He noticed a subtle abrasion on one of the victim's hands, a detail that might be crucial later.

Ever the steady hand, Sergeant Miller began coordinating with his informants on the streets. His cynical wit and uncanny ability to read people made him invaluable in gathering information from the city's underbelly. He knew the importance of building trust and understanding the nuances of human behavior. He was more than just a sergeant; he was a connector, weaving together disparate threads of information to create a cohesive narrative.

Diaz's search yielded a small but potentially significant lead. One of the victims had made a sizeable online transaction just days before his disappearance. The recipient was untraceable, but the amount matched the fortune mentioned by the homeless woman. A glimmer of hope, however faint, pierced the darkness.

Just as they were about to start the meeting, the Mayor arrived, whispered to Ethan and joined the meeting.

"Guys, our Mayor would like to hear the updates directly from you," Ethan advised the team.

"Good evening, Ma'am." They chorused as the Mayor gave a gentle nod of appreciation.

The team assembled around a table in the squad room, the air thick with the unspoken tension of the investigation. The rain outside continued its relentless drumming, mirroring the storm of questions swirling in their minds: empty coffee cups and scattered files littered the table, a testament to their late-night work.

"The suits," Sergeant Miller began, his voice low and serious, "are a significant detail. Why would homeless men buy expensive suits? It's not like they were going to a job interview."

Officer Diaz nodded, his fingers still tapping rhythmically on his laptop. "And the online transaction. The amount is significant, and the recipient is untraceable. It's like they vanished into thin air, just like the victims."

Dr. Ramirez, ever meticulous, pointed to a detail in the coroner's report. "The abrasion on the victim's hand...it's too clean, too precise. Not like a typical struggle. It's almost...surgical."

Sarah Chen, ever practical, chimed in. "The press release needs careful wording. We can't confirm anything yet but must acknowledge the public concern. Any premature statements could fuel panic and hinder the investigation."

Ethan leaned back, his gaze sweeping across his team. "We have puzzle pieces," he stated, "but the picture is far from complete. The suits suggest a disguise, and the money points to a motive, and the clean abrasion hints at a calculated act. But what connects it all? Who receives that money, and what is their connection to the victims?"

Sergeant Miller tapped a photo of one of the victims. "Maybe they were all part of something bigger. A gang? A secret society? Something we don't even know about yet."

A long silence followed, punctuated only by the drumming rain. The questions outweighed the answers, the possibilities endless and unsettling. The investigation was far from over; it had only just begun.

The team meeting finished late into the night, and the weight of the investigation was pressing down on everyone. The rain outside had intensified, relentlessly drumming against the windows. As Ethan and Ysabel prepared to leave, the shared intensity of their collaboration created an undeniable spark.

Ethan offered to drive Ysabel home. The drive was silent, punctuated only by the rhythmic swish of the wipers and the drumming rain. By the time they reach Ysabel's apartment building, both are soaked to the bone, their clothes clinging to them, their hair plastered to their foreheads.

Ysabel hesitated at the doorway, a fleeting thought crossing her mind. She turned to Ethan, a hint of something unspoken in her eyes. "The rain...it's coming down hard," she said softly, her voice barely audible above the storm. "Perhaps you should come inside?"

Ethan's gaze meets hers, his own emotions mirroring hers. But a sudden thought of Lily, his daughter, alone with the babysitter, stops him. He shakes his head gently, a hint of regret in his voice. "Perhaps another time," he says, "I wouldn't want to leave Lily alone."

He offers a small, almost shy smile. "Rain check?"

Ysabel smiles back, a bittersweet expression that speaks volumes. "Rain check," she echoes softly, her gaze lingering on his face.

As Ethan drove away, the rain continued to fall, a relentless backdrop to the unspoken emotions that lingered between them. Both were left with a lingering sense of what might have been, the unspoken feelings between them growing stronger with each passing moment. The rain washed away the grime of the day but not the intensity of their shared experience or the growing attraction that hung in the air between them.

4

Shadows and Suspects

The investigation into the missing persons seemed to hit a wall. To Councilman Ricardo Alvarez, the ambitious Vice-Mayor, remained a prime suspect. His ostentatious lifestyle and apparent animosity toward Mayor Ashworth raised suspicions, but a thorough investigation yielded nothing concrete linking him to the money laundering scheme. His financial records were impeccable, and his alibi was airtight. He was, frustratingly, a dead end—or so it seemed.

Ethan, however, decided to invite Alvarez for questioning. He presented Alvarez with a printout of suspicious transactions, as the Anti-Money Laundering Division (AMLD) reported. Based on bank reports, the transactions exceeded the threshold amount under AMLD rules and regulations. The printout was a collection of seemingly unrelated transactions, yet all directly or indirectly linked to Alvarez.

Despite the evidence, Alvarez vehemently denied any involvement in money laundering. He was calm, collected, and even charming under pressure. He argued that the transactions were related to legitimate business dealings, offering plausible explanations for each one. The money laundering scheme has not yet been identified; the transactions were suspicious but not definitively linked to any illegal activity.

Just as Ethan was about to press further, Alvarez's lawyer arrived, a stern-faced woman with a sharp wit and an even sharper legal mind. She immediately instructed Alvarez not to answer any more questions without her present. Bound by legal procedure, Ethan had no choice but to release Alvarez without filing charges.

While the Alvarez lead proved fruitless, a new one emerged—a homeless man named Michael, who recently purchased a house in cash. He claimed to have inherited much money from a deceased grandmother. The timing was suspicious—about a week before the disappearances, coinciding with the three men buying suits. Furthermore, Michael had invited several friends to stay with him, including the woman who contacted Ysabel. The team began investigating Michael, but their initial inquiries yielded nothing conclusive. The inheritance seemed legitimate, as was the house purchase above board.

However, something felt off, a nagging sense of unease that prevented them from dismissing Michael as just another homeless man who suddenly came into a fortune. The team realized that the trial was deliberately misleading, and each lead was carefully constructed to throw them off the scent of the true culprit. The money laundering and the missing persons were connected, but the connection was far more complex and dangerous than they initially realized. The investigation was far from over.

Exhausted, Ethan drove home, the weight of the unsolved case pressing down on him. The unresolved investigation was a heavy burden, but it was nothing compared to the turmoil in his personal life. His daughter, Lily, was becoming increasingly rebellious, her anger and resentment towards him growing daily. She blamed him for her mother's death, a guilt he carried silently, a wound that refused to heal. He knew he needed to find a way to connect with her, to mend the broken pieces of their relationship before it was too late. The chapter ends with Ethan staring at Lily's bedroom door, the silence amplifying the unspoken tension between them, starkly contrasting the complex investigation unfolding around him.

5

A Legacy of Courage

Ysabel's phone vibrated, and she saw Ethan's name and number on caller ID. The conversation was initially about scheduling a meeting, but it quickly veered towards a more personal tone.

"Ethan, I'm swamped. This investigation is consuming me. And the Council... they're not making things easier. I could really use a break."

Ethan replied softly, "I know. It's been intense. Maybe... dinner? To unwind? My treat. We could talk about something other than missing persons."

Ysabel whispered a small laugh, "I'd like that. How about tomorrow night? Somewhere quiet."

"Perfect," Ethan replied, unable to hide his excitement. "I'll make a reservation. I know a place with a great view."

"Sounds lovely," Ysabel was equally excited. "I look forward to it, Ethan."

They hang up, a lingering feeling of anticipation in the air for both of them.

Ethan arrived at the restaurant first. He sat at a window table overlooking the awe-inspiring sunset on the horizon. He also can see the door. A few minutes later, Ysabel entered the restaurant in a red, flowing dress that hung just a few inches above the knee, displaying her long legs. She was carrying a small red Louis Vitton bag and a simple pearl necklace, accentuating her whole countenance. Ethan thought his heart skipped a bit. After recovering his composure, he stood up and greeted Ysabel. He kissed her lightly on the cheek, and they sat down on their chairs.

Some patrons bowed to the Mayor, who courteously returned to acknowledge with a bow and a smile. She was radiant.

The atmosphere was relaxed yet charged with unspoken tension. They made small talk initially, but the conversation gradually turned more profound.

Ethan: So, tell me about your family. You're fiercely independent, but a story must be behind that.

Ysabel smiled faintly and replied with much hesitation. My family history is… quite something. It's a story of courage and resilience. It all started with my great-great-grandfather.

Ysabel paused, looking out at the ocean with a wistful expression. Ethan watched her, captivated by her quiet intensity.

Ethan looked at her with much admiration, "I'm listening."

Ysabel took a deep breath, ready to share a significant part of her history. A meaningful glance was exchanged between them before she began her story

The year is 1820, a couple of decades before the signing of the Treaty of Waitangi. New Zealand was a divided land, with various tribes vying for power and control. Manakitanga Island, nestled between Patikirau Bay and Cox Bay, is a small but prosperous island led by the renowned Chieftain Wiremu Heni. His leadership has brought great progress to his people, sparking envy among neighboring tribes.

One such tribe, driven by greed and ambition, attacked Manakitanga Island. They planned their assault from the east, believing that the island's warriors would expect an attack from the west, the more accessible side. However, Chieftain Wiremu Heni, a shrewd strategist, anticipated this and made a bold move. He appointed George Patrick Ashworth, an Englishman who had earned the chieftain's trust through his loyalty and skill, as his right-hand man.

GP Ashworth and 300 local warriors were tasked with defending the eastern cliffs—a seemingly impossible task, given the sheer number of attackers. The battle was fierce. The volcanic stones across the beach became weapons and obstacles, adding to the chaos. The air was thick with the smell of blood and the cries of the dying. GP Ashworth, outnumbered but undaunted, displayed extraordinary courage and leadership. He positions his men on the cliffs, using the high point to their advantage, picking off the enemy with arrows. Many fell on both sides, and the volcanic stones soon stained crimson.

Despite being wounded multiple times, GP Ashworth's bravery inspired his men. They fought with unwavering determination, repelling wave after wave of attackers. The battle raged for hours, a testament to the courage and resilience of the defenders. Finally, exhausted but victorious, GP Ashworth and his men emerged triumphant. The shores were littered with the bodies of the enemy, a stark reminder of the battle's ferocity.

In recognition of his extraordinary courage and leadership, Chieftain Wiremu Heni gave GP Ashworth the greatest honor—the hand of his only daughter in marriage. This union symbolized a personal triumph and a testament to the growing unity and respect between the settlers and the Indigenous people.

As Ysabel concluded her story, a poignant silence hung in the air. Ethan was deeply moved by her account, recognizing the parallels between her ancestor's courage and her strength in the face of her current challenges. Their shared experience created a more profound connection, strengthening the bond that had developed since they began working together.

6

A Shared Burden – Unveiling the Past

The lingering silence after Ysabel's story hung heavy in the air. The emotional resonance of her great-great-grandfather's tale created a deeper connection between her and Ethan. The quiet intimacy of the restaurant, the soft glow of the candlelight, and the gentle lapping of waves against the shore created a perfect backdrop for the vulnerability that followed.

Captivated by her story and the strength it revealed, Ethan found himself drawn to her in a way he hadn't anticipated. He felt a sudden urge to reciprocate and share his burdens and vulnerabilities. He reached across the table, his hand briefly brushing hers, a silent acknowledgment of the unspoken connection growing between them.

Ethan whispered, eyes not leaving hers, "Ysabel, your story... it was incredible. Your family's legacy of courage is truly inspiring. It makes me wonder... why aren't you married? You seem capable of anything."

Ysabel's smile faded slightly, and her eyes showed a hint of sadness. She took a sip of water, gathering her thoughts before responding.

She replied, "It's complicated, Ethan. There was Liam... We were deeply in love, but... he died. It was a slow, painful death. We were on a rescue mission for some of our men holed up in enemy territory. It was a dangerous mission, but our intel was solid. However, we were ambushed along the way, and half of my team, including Liam, was lost. It left a void in my life that I couldn't fill. I've always focused more on my career and serving this city. Building a life with someone else... it feels impossible."

"A Copy of Poetry?"

Ysabel's eyes looked at Ethan's and they both understood that there were things left nsaid.

A long silence hung between them, broken only by the sound of the waves. Ethan's gaze softened; his eyes filled with empathy. The pain in Ysabel's voice resonated deep within him.

Ethan said quietly, almost in a whisper, "I understand loss. I lost Lily's mother, Sarah... in a car accident. I was driving. I was drunk." He paused, his voice thick with emotion. "It's a burden I'll carry for the rest of my life. The guilt... it's a constant companion." His voice was broken like a lump in his throat, and he could not speak.

Ethan looked away, unable to meet Ysabel's gaze. The revelation hung in the air, a shared wound that unexpectedly connected them.

A long, comfortable silence settled between them, punctuated only by the gentle sounds of the ocean. Their hands remained clasped, a silent attestation to their shared burden and nascent connection.

Suddenly, Ethan's phone rang, shattering the intimate moment. He excused himself, answering the call with a grim expression. The conversation was brief but urgent. He hung up, his face etched with concern.

"Ysabel, I'm so sorry, but we need to go. It's about Michael," Ethan said with urgency.

He stood up, pulling out his chair to help her up. Their eyes met, and their hands lingered longer than necessary before leaving the restaurant.

They rushed to the police war room, the romantic atmosphere replaced by the urgent pulse of the investigation. Ethan's IT guy, David, was waiting, his face illuminated by the glow of multiple computer screens. He presented them with a stunning revelation: Michael's story, inheritance, and identity—all meticulously fabricated. "He's not who he claims to be. Instead, he's a small but significant player in a vast identity theft scheme," David said confidently. The discovery put the investigation in a new, more complex direction, leaving Ysabel and Ethan to realize that the seemingly simple case of missing persons has become exponentially more dangerous.

7

Web of Deceit – Unraveling the Identity Theft

The war room buzzed with tension as David leaned over the computer screen, his fingers dancing across the keyboard. The monitor's glow illuminated his face, revealing a mix of determination and concern. Ethan and Ysabel stood nearby, their eyes fixed on the screen as David prepared to reveal his findings.

Turning to them, his voice steady, David said softly, "I've been digging into Michael's background, and what I found is alarming. It looks like he's part of a much larger identity theft ring targeting residents of rest homes."

Ethan frowned, "Targeting rest homes? How does that work?"

Pointing at the screen, Davin explained, "These criminals specifically choose elderly individuals who have no known relatives. When one of them dies, a person—like Michael—claims to be a relative. They came in with a lawyer and comprehensive documents that looked legitimate. They'll have fake IDs and birth certificates, you name it."

Ysabel was intrigued. She crossed her arms and enquired, "And how do they pull this off?"

"It's a well-oiled machine," David nodded. "They meticulously replaced all records of a relative who died long before with new records for the replacement, such as Michael. They often recruit from the homeless population, people who are desperate for money and a fresh start. Michael, it seems, was one of those whom they approached."

Ethan's curiosity heightened. He asked, "So, what happens after they claim the inheritance?"

David leaned closer to the screen and said, "Once they're in, they gain access to everything—stocks, investments, overseas accounts—all under the guise of a Special Power of Attorney. But here's the kicker: once they have control, they vanish. The crime group takes everything, leaving the recruited individuals with a small payout—sometimes just enough to keep them quiet."

They all looked at each other, amazed by the complexity of the hoax. "But why would Michael come back to Red Stones City? He bought a house in cash, which seems risky," Ethan asked.

"That's the strange part," David said. "It's like he thought he could escape their watchful eyes. The crime syndicate doesn't take kindly to rule-breakers. They usually eliminate anyone who poses a threat to their operation."

Ethan's jaw was tightening. "If they find out he's back and spending their money, he'll be in grave danger."

Ysabel added, "We need to find out more about this syndicate and what they're planning. If Michael is involved, we might be able to uncover a larger operation."

As the tension in the war room began to settle, David glanced at the clock on the wall, realizing it was time to call it a night.

David stretched his tired arms and excused himself, "I think I've done enough digging for one day. I'll update you if I find anything else on Michael or the syndicate."

"Thanks, David," Ethan and Ysabel chorused in approval. "We appreciate your hard work."

With a knowing smile, David winked and said, "Just don't stay too late. You two need to figure this out."

With that, David gathered his things and left the room, his footsteps echoing down the hallway. The door clicked shut, leaving Ethan and Ysabel alone in the dim light of the office.

A heavy silence enveloped them, the weight of the day's revelations hanging in the air. They stood facing each other, their eyes locked, both acutely aware of the unspoken tension that had been building between them.

Ethan's heart raced as he searched Ysabel's gaze, sensing her conflicted feelings mirrored in his own. For a brief moment, they hesitated, the world outside fading away, leaving only the two of them in this charged space.

Ysabel whispered, "Ethan..."

Ethan took a step closer, "Ysabel, I—"

Before he could finish his thought, something shifted. The intensity of their shared experiences, the pain of their pasts, and the urgency of the present collided at that moment. They moved towards each other, and before they knew it, their lips met in a soft, tentative kiss that quickly deepened, fueled by desire and longing.

In that kiss, they found solace from their struggles, a fleeting escape from the chaos surrounding them. The world around them disappeared, leaving only the warmth of their connection, the beating of their hearts synchronized in a rhythm that felt both new and familiar.

As they finally pulled away, breathless and lost in each other's eyes, they knew this moment was just the beginning—a spark igniting a flame that would carry them through the challenges ahead.

8

The Street's Whisper – A Network Unfolds

The investigation into the missing persons and the burgeoning identity theft ring was far from a solo act. While Ethan and Ysabel focused on the high-level aspects of the case, Sergeant Miller, a seasoned detective with an unparalleled network of informants on the streets, worked tirelessly to gather intelligence from the city's underbelly. His years of experience and deep understanding of the city's hidden currents proved invaluable.

Miller's approach was methodical, and his network was extensive. He spent his days and nights weaving through back alleys, coffee shops, and dimly lit bars, cultivating relationships with informants who shared crucial information. His network was a tapestry of whispers and rumors, a mosaic of insights from seemingly disparate sources.

One evening, while sitting at a local diner, Miller struck up a conversation with a couple of fishermen. They shared a wild story about a small plane they had witnessed dropping something into the ocean off the island's eastern side.

The first fisherman leaned in and, with his eyes wide with excitement, said, "I swear, we saw it! A small plane just above the water dropped packets. It was around dawn, and then a speedboat came out of nowhere, scooped them up, and vanished near the marina.

"Did you catch a glimpse of the boat or anything else?" Miller asked.

The second fisherman shook his head apologetically, "It was just the speedboat. But it was quick like it was on a mission."

This information thrilled Miller. He confirmed their sighting with the state witness, who revealed that those packets were smuggled from South America, often linked to the drug and gun trade.

Miller continued digging deeper, seeking connections to tie these new developments to the yacht club. One of his informants, a waiter at a bar near the marina, provided an unexpected lead.

The waiter nervously glanced around and whispered, "I once served drinks at the yacht club for a private event. I overheard some of the members talking about shipments—drugs and guns being brought onto the island and distributed out to parts of New Zealand."

"Did they mention anything specific? Shipments, schedules?" Miller was curious.

"Nah. Not really. They were talking about deliveries coming in every few weeks. I think they have a whole operation set up," the waiter continued.

As Miller pieced the puzzle together, the connections became clearer. The drugs and weapons were being smuggled into the island and distributed all over New Zealand, and the money was laundered through the casino owned by one of the officers in the yacht club's inner circle. It was a web of deceit that extended far beyond what he had imagined.

Returning to the police station, he gathered his findings into a comprehensive report. Each thread of evidence pointed toward a sophisticated and ruthless operation that exploited the island's beauty while hiding its darkest secrets.

Miller knew they were on the verge of a significant breakthrough. The discovery of the smuggling operation and the connection to the yacht club opened new avenues for investigation, and he was determined to bring the criminals to justice.

One informant, a former associate of the three deceased men who bought suits, revealed details about their activities. Another, a disgruntled employee of a local casino, corroborated the information about the money-laundering scheme. But the most significant lead came from a disgruntled former yacht club member, who had grown disillusioned with the inner circle within the club.

Now a state witness, this informant provided critical information about the yacht club's inner circle—members who were fully aware of their involvement in various parts of the crime ring. They were not just socialites but complicit players in a game that spanned far beyond the club's lavish parties. Miller validated the informant's claims, cross-referencing details with his other sources, and the pieces began to fit together.

The informant had been placed in a safe house, protected under police watch. Miller knew that time was of the essence; the syndicate would likely be looking for him to silence him. He compiled his findings into a comprehensive report, detailing the money-laundering operation, the identity theft scheme, and the key players involved, including the names of those in the yacht club's inner circle.

Returning to the police station, Miller gathered his findings into a comprehensive report. Each thread of evidence—the fishermen's sighting, the state witness's testimony, the waiter's overheard conversation—pointed toward a sophisticated and ruthless operation that exploited the island's beauty while hiding its darkest secrets. He knew they were on the verge of a breakthrough. The discovery of the smuggling operation and the connection to the yacht club opened new avenues for investigation, and he was determined to bring the criminals to justice.

Miller presented the report to Ethan, who was both stunned and energized by the scope of the operation.

Miller leaned back in his chair, a satisfied grin on his face. "We've got a solid lead. This informant could blow the whole operation wide open."

Ethan, nodding, deep in thought, said, "We need to move quickly. We must ensure he stays protected while gathering more information if he's in a safe house.

Miller interjected, "And we should prepare for the possibility that the inner circle won't let this go without a fight. They'll want to keep their secrets buried."

Ethan and Miller strategized their next steps with a new resolve, knowing they were on the precipice of a significant breakthrough. The discovery of the yacht club as the crime ring's headquarters opened up a new world of possibilities, and they were determined to uncover the truth.

Armed with the new development, Ethan immediately called Ysabel.

Ethan said to Ysabel, "We have a major breakthrough. Miller uncovered a smuggling operation connected to the yacht club. It involves drugs, guns... the whole nine yards. It's bigger than we thought."

Ysabel sighed and replied, "Do we have names?"

Ethan sent it to her phone. "I'm on it. Give me a few minutes."

Ysabel hung up and immediately, accessed the city hall records, focusing on the yacht club and its members. She confirmed the names Miller had provided and cross-referenced them with other city records, looking for any inconsistencies or hidden connections. She worked quickly, and her efficiency and experience paid off.

Ysabel called Ethan back, her voice jumping with excitement, "Ethan, I've confirmed the names Miller gave you. I've also compiled files on five possible members of the crime ring. Meet me at our favorite restaurant. I've got something to show you."

While waiting for their lunch to be served at the restaurant, Ysabel handed Ethan a folder containing the files. She also pulled out her phone and made a call.

While Ethan was browsing the file, Ysabel called somebody. With her voice low and serious, she said, "Marcus, it's Ysabel. I need your help. We've uncovered a major drug smuggling operation linked to a yacht club here. It's likely connected to a South American cartel. I was hoping you could run some checks on these names." And she hung up. She mumbled, "Don't be surprised if the Vice Mayor's name pops up."

Ethan watched Ysabel, impressed. "Who's Marcus?"

Ysabel smiled faintly. "An old friend from the military. He's got connections at the Pentagon. He can help us trace the smuggling route and identify the cartel." There was a pause, and she smiled, "Did I hear jealousy in those words?"

The arrival of their lunch momentarily interrupted their conversation, but the anticipation of what lay ahead hung heavy in the air. They knew they were on the verge of something big, and the stakes were higher than ever.

9

Shadows of Conspiracy – A Gathering Storm

The opulent villa of the Vice Mayor stood majestically on a cliff overlooking the ocean. Inside, the air crackled with tension as five figures gathered in the main living room. It is very seldom that they meet at his villa. So, everybody expected a very serious meeting. Usually, they meet and discuss while playing golf at the Red Stones Island Golf Club.

The scene was a tableau of power and influence:

The Vice Mayor presided over the meeting, as he always does. His face was etched with a mixture of concern and determination. He was the apparent leader, but only he knew the true extent of the operation and the identity of the Man in the Shadows. He was short, just a little over five feet and ten inches. But he had a commanding presence whenever he entered a room; he seemed to occupy it. He loved dressing in white slacks and white shirts.

Then, to the Vice Mayor's right, was the General Manager of the Bank of Manakitanga, Red Island City Branch. He's considered a pillar of the city's financial establishment, his presence lending an air of respectability to the gathering. Rimless glasses perched on his upturned nose. He talked a lot.

To the left of the Vice Mayor was the owner of the only Casino on the Island. He was known to be a shrewd businessman with a reputation for ruthlessness. His eyes scanned the room like he was looking for a cheater on a baccarat table. He was six feet tall, with muscular tones in his well-built body.

Further to the right of the Vice Mayor, the President of the Red Stones Island Yacht Club sat quietly. He was a charismatic figure with a network of influential connections, his smile concealing a calculating mind. He seldom talked, but when he did, people listened. He's married to a beautiful young woman, which he carries like a trophy.

Finally, on the far left of the Vice Mayor was the Entrepreneur Extraordinaire. He owns many businesses in the country and on the island, including a trucking company called QuickDucks Moving Company.

The Vice Mayor called the meeting to order. "Gentlemen, let's dispense with pleasantries. I sense something is off. There is a growing unease in the city. The police seem to be closing in. I've felt it for weeks. Let's hear individual reports. Ellie, start us off."

The Bank Manager, Ellie Hayes, knew she'd always called first to give updates on his operations. He came prepared. He said, "We washed our monies efficiently. The casino remains our primary conduit, but we're diversifying to minimize risk. Everything's within acceptable parameters. We are ready to increase our productivity."

The Owner of the Casino leaned back with a smirk playing on his lips. "We had minor hiccups, but nothing that we cannot handle. We're always cautious. Our clientele remains loyal, and our operations are flexible enough to handle more volume."

The Vice Mayor smiled. He looked at Wally Higgins, the President of the Yacht Club, calmly lighting his cigarette. He was in charge of logistics.

His report was just as quick but covered the essentials. "Deliveries are on time, and distribution is efficient. Our contacts in South America are reliable, and shipments are arriving as scheduled. Quick-

Ducks ensures seamless distribution and timely collection," he said quickly. "We are expecting our partner overseas that they will increase productivity in the next few weeks. We are looking at a very profitable year ahead. Logistics are flawlessly handled. We have expanded our fleet and optimized routes to minimize detection. No problems to report."

The Vice Mayor said calmly, "Excellent. Now, Intelligence." He paused, glancing towards the side office where the Man in the Shadows remained unseen. His rhythmic cigar-puffing became more frequent, signifying discomfort.

"Our inside man in the Mayor's office reported that the Mayor suspected something fishy in the dead bodies found in the river the other day. An investigation is in full swing," the Vice Mayor tried to sound confident. "But they have no leads."

He continued, "But I still feel uneasy. This investigation is escalating. We need to be prepared. Proactive."

The Casino Owner scoffed, "Nonsense, Victor. We're too well-connected to be caught. Our influence runs deep."

The Bank General Manager added, "Our operations are carefully structured. We've covered our tracks meticulously. There's nothing to worry about."

Ignoring the others' reassurances, the Vice Mayor continued, "We need to be ready for anything. This isn't just a minor investigation. I have a feeling this is bigger than we initially thought. Much bigger. I've noticed something else... a brewing relationship between the Mayor and the Police Inspector. It's subtle, but it's there.

"And what's your point, Victor?" the Casino Owner asked.

The Vice Mayor quipped, "My point is, we need to neutralize them. Take them off the board. I propose we take the offensive. I believe a deepfake is sufficient in the meantime. This will divert their attention and keep all their resources busy."

The Bank General Manager's widened in disbelief, "A deepfake? Are you serious?"

The Vice Mayor retorted, "Dead serious. A convincing fake video of the Mayor in a compromising position. It doesn't even have to be with the Inspector. Just something scandalous enough to derail the investigation. It'll throw them off our trail."

The Yacht Club owner asked, "And who will create this deepfake? This requires a high level of skill and discretion."

The Casino owner leaned forward, a predatory gleam in his eyes. "I have the right man for the job – a "black hat" in my casino. He's a master of the digital world. He can make a video so realistic that no one will ever suspect it's fake. And no one will ever trace it back to us."

The Entrepreneur Extraordinaire voiced his concerns about the deepfake. "But this is too risky if it's discovered. Looks like a tempest in a teacup for me."

The Vice Mayor cut him off, "The risk is worth it. It's a calculated gamble. It's better to be proactive than reactive. This will buy us time to consolidate our operations, eliminate loose ends, and prepare for whatever comes next."

The weight of the Vice Mayor's words hung heavily in the air. The seemingly impenetrable web of influence they had carefully constructed was now threatened. The Man in the Shadows, unseen but ever-present, remained silent, his cigar a constant reminder of the power and danger that lurked beneath the surface. The meeting ended with an unspoken tension, a shared sense of foreboding, and a new, dangerous plan taking shape.

10

The Banker's Gambit – A Web of Deceit

The early morning sun filtered through the tall windows of Ellie Hayes's office, casting long shadows across the room. Papers were strewn across his desk, a chaotic reflection of his mind. He picked up his phone and dialed a familiar number, his heart racing as he waited for the call to connect.

The Bank Manager's voice was low, "It's me. I need to warn you. There's chatter in the wind—something's brewing within the crime ring. They suspect you might be too close to the police."

The mayor replied just as low, "Thank you for the heads-up. I'll be careful. What else do you know?"

Ellie sighed, "Just watch your back. I can't say much, but I'll keep you posted."

As they ended the call, the Mayor sat on her chair, looked out at the horizon and asked her secretary to call Ethan.

"Yes, Mayor," the secretary quickly exited to fulfill her duties.

"Ma'am, the Police Inspector on line 1," and the Mayor picked up the phone.

"Ethan, I just received a warning from the Ellie Hayes. She feels a growing threat from the crime ring, and we need to be on high alert. It looks like our window is closing fast."

"I suspected as much," Ethan replied. "Why does that name sound familiar?" Ethan asked himself.

Meanwhile, Ellie Hayes hung up the phone, her mind racing. She gathered herself, focusing on the scattered folder on the table. It contained reports detailing the money-laundering operation, and she needed to prepare for a special meeting with her inner circle—those selected few who were aware of the laundering scheme.

In a dimly lit conference room, the bank manager addressed her trusted associates, each a key player in the laundering operation, saying, "We have a situation. Three bodies were found from our last operation. They started a spending spree that drew too much attention and were eliminated.

The Head of Operations asked nervously, "What about the next batch? When's it coming in?"

Ellie confidently replied, "In two weeks. This one will be the biggest yet—about $100 million. We need to spread it across all casinos in the country, including ours on the island.

The Head of Operations inquired, "And what about the Casino Kingpin?"

Ellie Hayes immediately replied, "He should be given advance information. We can't afford any slip-ups."

As the meeting continued, Ellie Hayes detailed the operations of their money-laundering scheme.

She explained, "The dirty money is dropped in packets into the ocean, then picked up by our contacts. It's distributed to the casinos and deposited into shell accounts. It's a well-oiled machine."

One Associate was cautious, "How do we avoid detection?"

Ellie smirked, "We add layers. We have shell accounts that funnel money to offshore banks, and then it's redeposited to the Bank of Manakitanga, our branch here on the island.

Another Associate was concerned, "What if something goes wrong?"

Ellie quickly replied, "That's why I'm implementing our exit plan. I'm rerouting the money for our safety—what I call "insurance." If things go south, we'll have options."

At the end of the meeting, Ellie Hayes felt a mix of anxiety and determination. She had to ensure that their operation ran smoothly while safeguarding her interests. With a final glance at the scattered reports, she knew the stakes had risen. She had to stay one step ahead of the crime ring and the authorities to survive.

As she left his office, her phone buzzed with a news alert. He clicked on the notification, his blood running cold as he read the headline: "Viral Video Rocks City Hall: Mayor in Scandal?"

The article detailed a scandalous video that had gone viral, showing the Mayor in a compromising situation. The footage was grainy, and the details were unclear, but the implications were devastating. The article speculated about a possible cover-up and called for a full investigation.

Ellie Hayes felt a chill run down his spine. She wasn't sure who to trust anymore. Everyone was playing their own game, and the stakes were higher than ever.

She looked at the scattered reports on her desk, a symbol of the precarious position she found herself in. She had to act fast before the situation spiraled completely out of control. She had to protect herself, her position, and her future. The news report was a stark reminder that the game was far from over. The war had just begun.

11

The Casino King - High Stakes and High Risks

The sun dipped low on the horizon, casting a golden hue over the island. The Casino Owner, Vincent "Vince" Malone, leaned against the balcony railing of his penthouse suite, taking in the breathtaking view of the sunset. It was a view that had become his trademark, a backdrop to the empire he had built from the ground up.

Fifteen years ago, Vince had arrived on Red Stones Island—a man with nothing but ambition and a knack for persuasion. He remembered the day the casino project had been proposed, a turning point in his life. It had been a gamble, but he had connected with the right people, navigating the murky waters of the underworld with the same confidence he had shown in high school, where he had scammed his classmates with card tricks.

Vince said to himself, with a smirk on his lips, "Who would've thought those card tricks would lead me here?"

His thoughts drifted to his past, the family he had lost in a tornado that had struck their home in the central states. He was the only survivor, having been in Las Vegas that fateful night, gambling away the last of his childhood. The insurance money had given him a fresh start, and he had seized the opportunity to create a new life on the island.

As he prepared for the evening's operations, Vince felt a familiar thrill. The casino had become his domain, where he wielded power and influence. With an astute sense of business and an understanding of the underworld, he transformed the establishment into a hub for high rollers and those looking to escape their troubles.

Vince gathered his inner circle in a private room at the casino. The atmosphere was charged with anticipation, and the stakes were high as they discussed their operations.

Vince leaned on his table, looked at his trusted men, and asked, "So, what's the status on the next batch?"

The Head of Operations was nervous but gathered enough courage to speak, "We're ready to move in two weeks. The plan is solid, but we must ensure we're not drawing attention this time."

Vince nodded in agreement, "I want everything smooth. We can't afford any mistakes. The last thing we need is the Mayor or the police to catch wind of this."

As they discussed logistics, Vince felt a rising sense of unease. The news of a viral video involving the mayor had spread like wildfire, and he knew it could have repercussions for their operations.

Vince frowned, "We need to keep our heads down. This scandal could bring unwanted scrutiny. If the authorities start digging, we'll all be in hot water."

Another Associate was anxious. He asked, "What if they connect the dots back to us?"

With a steely resolve, Vince said, "That's why we must be cautious. We've built this empire, and I won't let it fall apart because of some viral video."

As the meeting concluded, Vince returned to his penthouse, the weight of his responsibilities heavy on his shoulders. He poured himself a drink, reflecting on his life. He had never married, preferring the company of the beautiful women who frequented the casino. They were a distraction, a way to fill the void left by his family.

Vince said, "Who needs love when you have everything else?"

But as he gazed at the horizon, he couldn't shake the feeling that something was shifting. The stakes were higher than ever, and he needed to be ready for whatever came next.

Vince poured himself another drink, the amber liquid swirling in the glass mirroring the turmoil in his mind. He needed reassurance, a guarantee that the deepfake wouldn't come back to haunt him. He activated the hidden intercom in his penthouse suite.

"Marco," he said, his voice low and controlled, "come up."

A moment later, Marco, his IT guy, entered. Lean, pale, with eyes that darted nervously, he was a master of the digital dark arts, a specialist in anonymity and deception.

Vince gestured to a chair. "Sit. I need to know, absolutely know, that this deepfake is untraceable. No loose ends. No digital fingerprints leading back to us."

Marco nodded, his fingers already tapping a silent rhythm on his thigh. "The video is clean, Mr. Malone. I used multiple layers of encryption and bounced it through several servers in different countries. It's virtually impossible to trace back to its origin. The algorithms I used are state-of-the-art and constantly evolving. It's practically undetectable."

Vince leaned forward, his gaze intense. "Practically isn't good enough, Marco. I need absolute certainty. One slip-up, and we're all finished."

Marco met his gaze, his expression unwavering. "Only if there's a better one than I am, Mr. Malone," he said, a hint of chilling confidence in his voice.

Meanwhile, in Ethan's dimly lit office, the air hung heavy with the weight of the newly discovered deepfake video. David, Ethan's IT guy, sat hunched over his computer, his face illuminated by the flickering screen. The grainy video, showing the Mayor in a compromising situation, played on a loop.

Ethan watched, his jaw tight. "It's well done," he admitted, "almost too good. The compression and the metadata have been scrubbed clean. Whoever did this knows his stuff."

David nodded grimly. "It's a professional job, no doubt. The level of sophistication suggests someone with extensive experience in deepfake technology. We're talking about someone who's not just skilled but also incredibly careful. They're covering their tracks meticulously."

Ethan ran a hand through his hair, frustration etching onto his features. "This changes everything. It'll throw the public off the scent, at least for a while. But it also means someone inside knows exactly what we're doing."

David tapped a few keys, a series of complex commands scrolling across the screen. "I'm trying to trace the video's path, but it's like trying to catch smoke. The encryption is robust, and the servers are all anonymized. It's a ghost in the machine."

Ethan stared at the screen, the implications of the deepfake sinking in. The investigation had just taken a dangerous, unpredictable turn. The game had escalated. David continued tapping on his keyboard. The better one was watching the deepfake.

12

The Shadow of David

The sterile glow of the computer screen illuminated Marco's face, a stark contrast to the warm, hazy memories that suddenly flooded his mind. The past was a shadow, always lurking just beyond the reach of the present, and tonight, it was closing in. Suddenly, he remembered his twin brother. The thought brought him to his past.

The squeak of polished leather against hardwood echoed in the cavernous hallway, a soundtrack to Marco's simmering resentment. He trailed behind David, the scent of his brother's freshly laundered polo shirt a constant, irritating reminder of their disparity. The trophy case gleamed under the harsh fluorescent lights, a veritable pantheon of David's achievements. Each polished surface reflected Marco's own frustrated image, a distorted mirror of inadequacy.

He remembered the awards ceremony and the crowd's roar as David accepted another trophy. He recalled his mother's cooing praise, "David, you're such a natural," her hand resting on his brother's shoulder. And his father's well-meaning but ultimately hollow words to him, "Marco, you just need to apply yourself more." The words were a constant, dull ache in his chest.

This constant feeling of inadequacy fueled his ambition, driving his relentless pursuit of technological excellence. He *would* show them. He *would* be the best.

But now, staring at the lines of code on his screen, a nagging doubt crept in. He saw David's influence, the subtle elegance of his programming style woven into his deepfake algorithm. The realization struck him like a physical blow.

Then, David's soft and clear voice cut through the haze of his memories: "You are excellent, bro. I am proud of you." The words hung in the air, a balm to his childhood wounds.

The image of David faded, replaced by the harsh fluorescent lights of his apartment. Vince's sharp and businesslike voice cut through the lingering warmth of David's praise. "Marco, I am proud of you." The calculated admiration grated on Marco.

He looked at the algorithm again, the elegant code now tainted by a sense of betrayal. A wave of exhaustion washed over him. The years of striving seemed pointless, and the validation felt hollow.

He thought of David, the quiet intensity in his eyes. The memory of David's pride starkly contrasted to Vince's cold ambition. The choice felt clear.

But caution ignited in his mind. Betraying Vince wouldn't be easy. He had seen Vince's ruthlessness.

Meanwhile, in a separate room, Vince paced restlessly. Guilt gnawed at him. He was trapped, and he saw no easy way out. He yearned for a different life, but he didn't know how.

His phone rang. He saw Ellie's name flash on the screen. He hesitated, then answered.

"Ellie," he said, his voice tight.

"Hi, Vince. Listen, I have a proposition..."

The rest of their conversation remained unspoken, hanging in the air, promising future complications and shifting alliances.

13

Fractured Trust

The city was in an uproar. News channels replayed the grainy video on an endless loop, the distorted image of Ysabel a stark contrast to the composed, confident mayor the city had come to know. Social media seethed with accusations; each comment a tiny shard of glass piercing her carefully constructed public persona. #MayorAshworthScandal trended globally, a wildfire fueled by speculation, accusations, and outright lies.

In her office, Ysabel slammed her fist on the desk, echoing the fury within her. The video was a blatant deepfake, a meticulously crafted piece of disinformation designed to discredit her and derail the investigation. Proving it, however, would be a Herculean task. The 24/7 news cycle, with its insatiable appetite for scandal, had already begun shaping public opinion. She picked up her phone, her fingers trembling slightly as she dialed Ethan's number. It went straight to voicemail. "Ethan," she left a message, her voice tight with a mixture of anger and despair, "meet me at the usual café. It's urgent."

Ethan switched off his phone to charge it. He forgot to charge it last night. The silence and absence of notifications, bells, and ringtones are unusual. Meanwhile, the constant buzz of calls was a jarring reminder of the chaos engulfing the city caused by the viral video of the Mayor. He knew the video was a fake. Still, the sheer volume of misinformation circulating online made him question whether he could convince anyone, even himself. His loyalty to Ysabel warred with his professional duty. He had to find the source of this deepfake, but the trail was deliberately obscured. He needed time and space to think. He needed to gather his thoughts before confronting Ysabel. He knew she was devastated.

He summoned David to his office. David burst in, his face alight with excitement. "I think I know who's behind it, boss! I mean I know who did it."

"What do you mean?" Ethan was surprised.

"The script and algorithm used looked familiar, and I remembered I taught it to my twin brother a long time ago," David explained.

"A twin brother?" Ethan could not hide his confusion.

"That's a talk for another day, boss."

The next day, Ysabel found Ethan at their usual café. The atmosphere was thick with unspoken tension. Ysabel launched into an explanation, her voice strained, "Ethan, I know you're angry, and you have every right to be. But this wasn't my doing. Someone is trying to sabotage us, to bring down the entire operation. I believe it's Vince Malone. He's been acting strangely."

Ethan stared at Ysabel, his mind reeling. Her confession was unexpected, a raw vulnerability that shattered the professional distance between them. He felt a surge of emotion – a complex mix of surprise, affection, and a deep sense of unease. The weight of the situation pressed down on him, making it hard to breathe. He opened his mouth to speak, but the words caught in his throat.

Before he could respond, Ysabel continued, her voice barely a whisper, "You know I love you, Ethan. There's nobody else, and you have to believe me."

The confession hung between them, a fragile bridge spanning the chasm of suspicion and uncertainty. Ethan's eyes softened, a flicker of hope igniting within him. But the weight of the situation remained, a heavy cloak draped over their burgeoning feelings.

Just then, his phone buzzed with a text from Ellie: "Meet me at the station. I've got a lead."

Ethan excused himself, leaning down to kiss Ysabel lightly on the cheek. "I'll be back," he murmured, his voice thick with emotion. He left Ysabel alone, the weight of the world pressing down on her shoulders.

At the station, Ellie's face was etched with determination.

Ellie leaned forward, her voice dropping to a whisper, "I know you are investigating on the money laundering and the three dead bodies found in the river. I know the risks. I've been playing a dangerous game, but I'm not a traitor. I can help you expose those responsible. I have information about the group and their next money-laundering operation. It's set for two weeks from now, and it's huge—about a hundred million dollars."

Ethan's heart pounded. This could be their chance to turn the tables. He looked at Ellie, a flicker of hope igniting in his eyes. But the image of Ysabel, alone and vulnerable in the café, lingered in his mind. The memory of Ysabel's confession hung heavy in the air, an unspoken promise amidst the chaos.

Ethan remained unconvinced. "Ellie, I need proof. I need to know I can trust you."

Ellie's eyes flickered with a mix of frustration and desperation. "I can't give you everything at once. It's too risky. But I can tell you this: the money will be laundered through the casinos. Vince is the key."

"How did you get this?" Ethan asked, his voice barely a whisper.

"From a friend," Ellie replied, her voice laced with a hint of bitterness, "a reliable one. One who doesn't leave without saying goodbye."

The unspoken words hung between them, a shared history of betrayal and regret. Ethan's gaze softened, his eyes filled with a mixture of guilt and understanding.

"Ellie," he began, his voice thick with emotion, "that was ages ago. I was young and stupid."

"Can we talk about it, some other time?" Ethan pleaded, his eyes searching hers.

"Of course," Ellie said, a hint of sarcasm in her voice, "let's focus on saving your *friend* first."

As Ellie was about to leave, she leaned and kissed Ethan on the cheek, just when Ysabel entered the room. Ellie and Ethan saw Ysabel standing at the doorway, her face a mask of uncertainty. Ellie was holding Ethan's hand, their intertwined fingers a silent testament to the complex web of relationships and betrayals that had entangled them. The tension in the air was palpable, the unspoken emotions hanging heavy between them—a silent acknowledgment of the fractured trust and the uncertain path ahead. The game had changed, and the stakes had never been higher.

"I thought you're my friend. How can you do this to me?" Ysabel screamed.

Ethan replied, "I still am, and I wll always be your friend."

"Not you. I'm talking to her," Ysabel pointed at Ellie.

"I am. There's nothing between us. It was in the past, and it's better left in the past," Ellie said.

"The past? You were, what?" Ysabel's voice was not a decibel higher.

Both Ellie and Ethan mumbled an explanation. The air was so intense that all three sat down and sighed.

"What a day," Ethan exclaimed.

14

Shadows of Betrayal

The Vice Mayor's office buzzed with tension as he leaned back in his chair, a storm brewing behind his steely gaze. He had just uncovered a troubling secret: Vince Malone, the notorious Casino Owner, may have been skimming money from their joint operations. The implications were serious, and the Vice Mayor felt the pressure mounting. He needed to act swiftly before Vince could cover his tracks.

He picked up the phone and dialed Travis Reed, his ambitious Head of Operations. "Travis, we need to talk," he said, his voice low and steady. I have a new contract for you. It's time to take over Vince's operations."

Travis's excitement crackled through the line. "You want me to take him out?"

"Precisely," the Vice Mayor replied, a dangerous edge to his tone. "I can't have loose ends. Vince's greed is a liability now. We need someone who can run the operation without question, and I think you're the right man for the job."

As they discussed the details, the Vice Mayor felt a power surge. This was his chance to solidify control, eliminate the competition, and assert dominance over the operation. But he did not know this decision would be his first grave mistake.

Later that night, as the moon cast a pallid glow over the city, Travis set his plan into motion. He and his men cornered Vince under a bridge, the river's dark waters lapping ominously below. The confrontation was swift and brutal; Vince never saw it coming. The last thing he felt was the cold steel of a blade against his skin as the world faded.

But fate had other plans. A group of teenagers wandering nearby stumbled upon the scene. They quickly called 111, and sirens pierced the night air within minutes. Vince was rushed to the hospital, clinging to life.

Meanwhile, believing he had successfully eliminated the competition, the Vice Mayor began to breathe easier. But the reality of the situation was more complicated. As the media reported that a "dead body" had been found under the bridge, purportedly cremated due to fears of biochemical infection, the Vice Mayor reveled in his perceived success, unaware of the storm brewing just below the surface.

Ethan received the call about Vince's condition while he was at the station. He rushed to the hospital, arriving just in time to witness the chaos unfolding. Doctors and nurses moved swiftly into the emergency room, but Ethan knew he couldn't let anyone know Vince was alive. He arranged to transfer Vince to a secured room where no one would be allowed access. The stakes had risen dramatically, and he had to keep this under wraps.

As the morning sun filtered through the hospital's sterile corridors, a flicker of movement in the secured room caught the nurse's attention. Vince Malone stirred, his eyes fluttering open. He looked around, confusion clouding his features. He remembered the attack, the cold steel of the blade, and then...nothing. He was alive.

Ethan, alerted by the nurse, rushed to the room. Vince's eyes met his, a mixture of relief and fear in their depths. "Ethan," Vince croaked, his voice weak, "they tried to kill me."

Ethan leaned closer, his expression hardened. "Who, Vince? Tell me everything."

And Vince did. He poured out the story of the Vice Mayor's greed, the contract, Travis Reed's ambition, and the skimming operation. He spoke of the intricate web of deceit, the money laundering scheme, and the identities of the conspirators. He recounted the details of the next shipment, the hundred million dollars waiting to be laundered. He spoke of Ellie's fears and her desperate attempt to warn Ethan.

Ethan listened intently, absorbing every detail. He knew he couldn't reveal Vince's survival to Ysabel yet. It would be too risky, placing Vince in further danger. He had to find out who leaked the deepfake video first. The insider was still out there, threatening both Vince and Ellie.

While Ethan was collecting his thoughts, he heard a knock on the door. It was Ellie. She had come to check on Vince. Seeing her fear, Ethan whispered, "Ellie, they tried to kill Vince. They'll come for you next."

Ellie's eyes widened, her face paling. "I knew it," she whispered, her voice trembling. "I have to get out of here."

Ethan nodded, a grim determination settling on his features. "We need to protect you both," he said, his gaze hardening. "We'll use this information to expose them all."

As Vince rested, his body still weak but his mind racing, Ethan and Ellie slipped out of the hospital, a silent pact forged between them. The Vice Mayor's escalation had backfired spectacularly, but the danger remained, and the game was far from over. Vince and Ellie were in mortal danger, and Ethan knew he had to move quickly. The weight of the situation pressed down on him, but he had a plan. Operation Medusa would begin immediately.

They reached Ethan's car, the night air thick with tension. Just as Ellie was about to slide into the passenger seat, the screech of tires shattered the silence. Two motorcycles roared into the parking lot, their riders clad in black leather, faces obscured by helmets. Before Ethan could react, a hail of bullets ripped through the air.

Ethan reacted instantly. Years of training kicked in, his body moving with practiced precision. He shoved Ellie behind him, his own body becoming a shield. He dove behind the car, returning fire with his own weapon. The sharp crack of gunfire echoed through the night, punctuated by the roar of the motorcycles and the screams of the attackers.

The firefight was short but brutal. Ethan's years of experience gave him a deadly advantage. He moved with a lethal grace, his shots precise and deadly. He took down one rider with a shot to the chest, then another with a shot to the head. The remaining two riders, realizing they were outmatched, attempted to flee. But Ethan was too quick. He took them down with two swift, accurate shots. The parking lot fell silent, the only sounds the heavy breathing of Ethan and Ellie and the distant wail of a siren.

Ethan checked Ellie for injuries. She was unharmed, but shaken. "We need to get out of here," he said, his voice low and urgent.

He helped Ellie into the car, then raced back to the secured room to retrieve Vince. He knew he couldn't leave Vince at the hospital. The Vice Mayor's men would be back. The hospital was no longer safe.

With Vince safely secured in the backseat, Ethan sped away, leaving the scene of the carnage behind. He drove to a secluded safe house, a well-hidden location known only to a select few. He knew they were still in danger, but here, they would be safer, at least for now.

As he watched Vince settle into the safe house, Ethan felt the weight of his responsibilities pressing down on him. He had to expose the Vice Mayor and his network, and he had to protect Vince and Ellie. The information Vince had provided was crucial, but it also put them all in the cross-hairs. Operation Medusa was more than just an investigation; it was a fight for survival.

15

The Call of Brotherhood

Marco stared at his reflection, the opulent surroundings of his apartment feeling cold and empty. The furrow in his brow mirrored the worry etched on his face. He ran a hand through his hair, the familiar gesture a small comfort in this moment of profound uncertainty. Vince's death had left him feeling exposed and vulnerable. Besides, he didn't like Travis. He missed his brother, David. The silence of the apartment pressed down on him, amplifying the loneliness.

He picked up his phone, his fingers hovering over Matthew's contact. Matthew Davidson, their mutual friend from High School, was among the few people who knew about his twin brother, David. He hesitated, then pressed the call button. Matthew answered, his voice casual, a stark contrast to the turmoil churning within Marco.

"Matthew, it's Marco," he began, his voice strained. "I need to talk."

He launched into a hesitant explanation of his situation, his voice tight with anxiety. Matthew listened patiently, offering words of comfort and encouragement. Long pauses punctuated their conversation, each silence heavy with unspoken anxieties.

"You need to talk to David, Marco," Matthew finally said, his voice gentle but firm. "He's your brother. He'll understand."

Marco hesitated. After all these years, the thought of contacting David filled him with hope and trepidation. But the longing in his voice betrayed his hesitation. "You're right," he whispered. "I need to talk to him."

He hung up, a glimmer of hope igniting in his eyes. He dialed David's number, his hand trembling slightly. David answered, his voice a familiar comfort. "Marco? Is that you?"

The initial exchange was filled with cautious pleasantries, but the underlying tension was palpable. Their shared history and close bond became evident as they began to talk. They finished each other's sentences, their thoughts seemingly intertwined.

Marco described the situation, his voice laced with desperation. David listened intently, his expression mirroring Marco's worry. They shared a moment of silence, a silent understanding passing between them. The same worried frown creased their brows, and the intensity flickered in their eyes.

"Remember when we tried to build a rocket in Mom's garage?" David chuckled, his voice laced with nostalgia.

"And it almost blew up?" Marco finished the sentence, a shared memory bringing a fleeting smile to his face.

They shared a joke, a moment of childhood innocence that highlighted the strength of their bond. Their identical mannerisms—the way they combed their hair and fidgeted with their hands—were subtle yet unmistakable.

As Marco revealed the dangerous dynamics at play, David's response was immediate and decisive. They brainstormed ideas, their thoughts meshing together, creating a plan to escape the Vice Mayor's control. Their identical expressions—a mixture of determination and fear—emphasized their connection.

"Where can we meet?" David asked his twin brother.

"How about the bar near the beach?"

"See you, then. By the way, Marco, I'm glad you called. I'm proud of you." David said.

16

Crumbling Control

The air in the Vice Mayor's dimly lit office hung thick with tension. Ricardo Alvarez, his face etched with a weariness that belied his usual confident façade, paced before Travis Reed and Wallace Higgins. The opulent room, usually a symbol of his power, felt claustrophobic, the shadows deepening the sense of unease.

"This... this isn't how it was supposed to go," Alvarez rasped, his voice betraying the tremor in his hands. The failed attempt on Ellie Hayes's life had left a gaping hole in their carefully constructed operation. The whispers of discontent among his underlings were growing louder, a constant, irritating buzz in the background.

Travis, ever the ambitious climber, remained outwardly confident. "We adjust, Ricardo. Malone's... absence creates an opportunity. I can take over his operations, consolidate—"

"Consolidate?" Alvarez cut him off, a harsh laugh escaping his lips. "You think this is a game of chess, Travis? This is a war, and we're losing." He slammed his fist on the mahogany desk, echoing in the oppressive silence. "Malone was a loose end, but now we have a bigger problem. The police are closing in. This deepfake... it was sloppy."

Wallace's usual charming demeanor replaced by a calculating stillness remained silent, his eyes fixed on Alvarez. He sensed the shift in the power dynamic, the cracks in the Vice Mayor's carefully constructed control. He knew instinctively that something far more dangerous was about to emerge.

A sudden, almost imperceptible click of the door echoed in the tense silence. A figure entered his silhouette a stark contrast against the dimly lit room. He was tall and imposing, his presence filling the space, yet his movements were fluid and almost silent. He wore a dark, impeccably tailored suit, his face obscured by shadows, but his eyes, sharp and intense, scanned the room, assessing each man with an unnerving precision.

The newcomer didn't speak, didn't need to. His presence radiated power, a chilling aura that completely silenced the room. Travis, his bravado momentarily faltering, shifted uneasily. Even Alvarez, accustomed to wielding power, felt a chill run down his spine.

Finally, the newcomer spoke, his voice a low, controlled baritone that resonated with an authority that dwarfed Alvarez's. "Ricardo," he said, the name a mere formality, devoid of any respect. "Your incompetence has become a liability."

The Man in the Shadows stepped further into the light, revealing a familiar yet unsettling face. It was a face Alvarez thought he knew, a face he had once trusted, a face that had been pulling the strings from the shadows all along.

"You assumed control, believing you could manage this operation alone. You were wrong." The Man in the Shadows' gaze swept over Travis and Wallace, his words carrying a weight that silenced any further protest. "This operation is far larger, far more intricate than you could ever comprehend. Your methods are crude, and your strategies are predictable. You've become a risk."

He paused, allowing his words to sink in, the silence punctuated only by Alvarez's ragged breathing. "I am here to correct your mistakes, ensure the operation continues uninterrupted, and eliminate any further threats to its success."

The power dynamic had irrevocably shifted. The Vice Mayor, once the undisputed leader, was now a mere pawn, his authority shattered, his future uncertain. Travis and Wallace exchanged nervous glances, their eyes reflecting a mixture of shock, awe, and a chilling premonition of what was to come. Having finally emerged from the darkness, the Man in the Shadows had taken control. The game had changed.

17

Unveiling Mr. K – The Past

The air in the dimly lit room, thick with the residue of fear and uncertainty from the previous night, had settled into a wary calm. Ricardo Alvarez, the Vice Mayor, sat rigidly in his chair, his usual confident demeanor replaced by a nervous stillness. Across from him, Travis Reed fidgeted his bravado from the night before and replaced it with a palpable unease. Wallace Higgins, ever the pragmatist, observed the scene with a calculating stillness, his eyes darting between the two men.

Then, he entered.

Sharneel Kumar—Mr. K—filled the doorway, his imposing figure casting a long shadow across the room. He was a mountain of a man, tall and heavy, his long, wavy hair swaying with a subtle twist of his head, a gesture both languid and commanding. His roots were Persian, his mother Indian, a blend reflected in his striking features. His black eyes, huge and intense, were like the headlights of a truck, almost comically disproportionate to his already massive head. Even in this tense moment, his vocabulary was laced with a casual vulgarity, his countenance more reminiscent of someone from the city's grittier underbelly than the sophisticated criminal mastermind he undoubtedly was.

"Alright, you lot," Mr. K boomed his voice a low rumble that resonated through the room. "I see the doubt in your eyes. You're wondering about me, about this... *change* in management. Let me assure you, this isn't some hostile takeover. This is a... *correction*."

He paused, letting his words hang in the air, allowing the tension to build before continuing. "To understand my decisions, you need to understand my past. It's a story of betrayal, loss, and the unwavering bond forged in the fires of adversity."

He leaned back in his chair, the leather creaking under his weight. His gaze swept across the room, lingering for a moment on each face before he began to speak, his voice taking on a softer, more reflective tone.

"It was the mid-80s. Kuala Lumpur. The air hummed with the energy of a city on the rise, but beneath the surface, a different kind of energy pulsed—the energy of illicit dealings, of stolen dreams sold for a pittance." He paused, his eyes distant, lost in the memories. "I was then, a cog in the machine, the assistant to the operations head of a massive DVD and CD piracy ring. We were moving millions, flooding the market with cheap, pirated copies—a small-time player in a vast, global empire."

He described the bustling streets, the hidden deals in dimly lit back alleys, and the constant fear of being caught. He painted a picture of his double life, the careful balancing act between his loyalty to his employers and his secret collaboration with Ricardo Alvarez, a Filipino CIA asset stationed in Malaysia.

"Alvarez... Ricardo," he said, a hint of something akin to reverence in his voice. "He was our ticket out. He saw the potential, the opportunity to dismantle this empire from the inside. We spent years planning, gathering intelligence, and building our case. We were going to bring them down."

His voice hardened, the casual vulgarity returning, edged with a deep, simmering rage. "Then came the raids. The overt operation. It went south faster than a greased piglet on a downhill slope. They burned my house down. My wife and my two children are gone. Reduced to ashes." His voice cracked, a raw vulnerability briefly piercing his tough exterior. "Ricardo found me, pulled me from the wreckage. He saved my life."

He paused, his massive head bowed, the silence heavy with unspoken grief. Then, he looked up, his eyes blazing with a cold, hard light. "That's the bond between us. A debt I can never repay. A loyalty that runs deeper than blood."

He straightened, his long hair swaying, the casual vulgarity returning to his voice, but now with a steely edge.

"So, this isn't about power grabs or personal vendettas. This is about continuity. About ensuring the operation continues uninterrupted. About finishing what we started. And about honoring the memory of my family by bringing down the very people who took them from me."

Mr. K paused, his gaze sweeping across the faces of his assembled associates. A strange calm settled over the room, a fragile peace born from a shared understanding of their past and common goals. The weight of his story, the raw emotion he'd poured into his confession, had broken through their initial skepticism, replacing it with a wary respect.

Just then, a sharp buzz cut through the heavy silence. It was Travis Reed's phone, the ringtone a jarring intrusion into the somber atmosphere. He glanced at the screen, his eyes widening in disbelief. He looked up, his voice a breathless whisper, "It's... it's breaking news."

He handed the phone to Wallace, who read the headline aloud: "Mayor Ashworth Considers Resignation Amid Deepfake Scandal."

A ripple of excitement ran through the room. The deepfake video, designed to discredit Mayor Ashworth and derail the investigation, had seemingly achieved its purpose. The news report, amplified across social media, painted a picture of a mayor under siege, her reputation in tatters. The crime ring, momentarily lulled into a false sense of security, felt a surge of triumph. Their scheme had worked. At least, that's what they thought.

Unknown to them, this "breaking news" was a carefully orchestrated maneuver, a strategic gambit in a much larger game. The resignation story, a carefully crafted piece of disinformation, was part of a PR campaign launched by Mayor Ashworth's team with the help of Sarah Chen, a brilliant PR expert who happened to be on Ethan's team. It was a calculated risk designed to lull the crime ring into a false sense of security, giving Ysabel, Ethan, Ellie, and Vince (assuming Vince's survival remains a secret) the time and space they needed to plan their next move.

The news report, however, served its intended purpose. It created a distraction, a moment of complacency within the criminal organization. While the members celebrated their perceived victory, Ysabel and Ethan, along with their unlikely allies, were already plotting their counterattack, their plans meticulously crafted, their resolve hardened by the knowledge that the fight was far from over. The game had just entered a new and far more dangerous phase.

18

Shifting Sands

The aroma of freshly brewed coffee hung in the air, a stark contrast to the dimly lit, smoke-filled rooms Marco was accustomed to. He sat across from his twin brother, David, their resemblance striking despite the differences in their lives. David, clean-cut and sharp in his police uniform, exuded an air of quiet competence. Still sporting his usual casual attire, Marco looked more like a seasoned gambler than a high-tech specialist. Yet, the years had only strengthened their bond, a shared history forging an unbreakable connection.

Their reunion, after years of separation, was filled with a mixture of relief and apprehension. They caught up on each other's lives, the conversation flowing easily, their thoughts and words complementing each other in a way only twins could understand. Marco's sharp wit and David's methodical approach had always been their strengths, and now, reunited, they were a force to be reckoned with.

But their conversation quickly turned to the grim reality of their opposing positions. Marco revealed his continued work for the crime ring, his decision to stay close to the action, to gather intelligence from within. "I'm their IT guy, David," he explained, a hint of grim satisfaction in his voice. I'll feed you information—in real-time. Everything they do, I'll know."

David listened, his expression a mixture of concern and admiration. He understood Marco's risks and moral compromises but also recognized the value of having an insider, a source of vital information that could bring down the entire operation.

"I don't like Travis," Marco added, his voice laced with contempt. "He's all bluster and no brains. He's missed the biggest opportunity of his life and doesn't even know it. He's focusing on the wrong things."

Meanwhile, a celebratory mood hung in the air in different parts of the city. Mr. K, Ricardo Alvarez, Wallace Higgins, and the other key members of the crime ring were gathered, their faces lit by the glow of expensive liquor and the promise of future power. Alvarez, the future mayor, was the center of attention, his ambitious plans for Red Stones City fueling their excitement.

"Once Alvarez takes office," Mr. K declared, his voice resonating confidently, "our opportunities will multiply. We'll expand our operations, consolidate our power, and become untouchable."

Oblivious to the growing unease within his own organization, Travis was already making plans for their next big move. "The big batch is ready," he boasted, his confidence bordering on arrogance. "We've recruited and vetted the new team. Homeless, no known relatives—perfect for the job. They're spread across the country, ready to move the goods."

He described the recruits, their new suits, and their instructions, his words painting a picture of an operation running smoothly and efficiently. He was unaware that his overconfidence had blinded him to the cracks forming within his ranks, Marco's insidious infiltration, and the meticulous planning of those about to bring his entire empire crashing down. The shifting sands of the criminal underworld were about to swallow him whole.

Meanwhile, a different kind of operation was underway in a quiet corner of Red Stones City. Ellie Hayes, her face etched with determination and apprehension, met with a homeless woman known only as "Maria." Maria, a sharp-witted survivor with a network of contacts throughout the city's underbelly, had provided vital information to the Mayor's team.

"Four men," Maria said, her voice low and urgent. "New recruits. Travis sent them to Auckland. Lots of cash. New suits. They're staying at the hotel near the beach on the island."

She described the men, their appearance, and their movements. She detailed how one of the men had visited her at the abandoned warehouse where they lived. He gave her lots of money for the rest of the friends.

This seemingly insignificant detail—four men buying new clothes in Auckland—was a crucial piece of the puzzle. It provided a tangible link between Travis's boastful claims and the reality of the crime ring's operations. It was a carefully laid breadcrumb leading directly to the heart of the criminal network.

The information was immediately relayed to Ethan, who, along with Ysabel, was already preparing their next move. The deepfake scandal, while a temporary setback, had bought them valuable time. Now, armed with Maria's intelligence, they were ready to strike. The shifting sands were not just threatening to swallow Travis; they were about to bury the entire criminal empire.

19

Operation Medusa

The midday sun streamed through the panoramic windows of the Mayor's office, illuminating the dust motes dancing in the air. Ysabel Ashworth, her face composed but her eyes sharp, addressed the assembled press. "Today, I can confirm that the recently circulated video depicting me in a compromising situation has been definitively identified as a sophisticated deepfake."

A collective sigh of relief rippled through the room. The scandal, which had threatened to derail her administration and undermine the ongoing investigation into the city's burgeoning criminal underworld, was finally laid to rest. Ysabel continued, her voice firm and confident. "The IP address of the individual responsible for uploading the video has been traced. While we are not yet ready to release the suspect's name, I assure you that a full investigation is underway and justice will be served."

The press conference concluded with a wave of positive news coverage. The deepfake crisis, a major obstacle, had been overcome. The city breathed a collective sigh of relief. But for Ysabel, the relief was short-lived. The real battle was far from over.

Later that afternoon, the atmosphere in her office was markedly different. Gone was the celebratory buzz of the press conference; in its place was a palpable tension. The same team—Ethan Cole, Sergeant

Miller, Officer Diaz and David Davies —were gathered around the mahogany table, the air thick with the scent of expensive coffee and unspoken anxieties. Ellie Hayes, her usual air of casual confidence slightly subdued, leaned against the wall, her eyes darting between Ysabel and Ethan.

"Operation Medusa is a go," Ysabel announced, her voice sharp and precise, cutting through the tension. "All contingencies are covered. We move at dawn."

Ethan nodded curtly, his gaze fixed on the briefing documents. The deepfake scandal had taken its toll, leaving him weary and on edge. The strain in his relationship with Ysabel was palpable, a silent acknowledgment of the recent turmoil.

"The timing is crucial," Ellie interjected, her voice smooth but laced with a subtle undercurrent of challenge. "The transfer of funds needs to happen precisely as planned. One wrong move and the whole operation collapses."

Ysabel's eyes narrowed. "We're aware of the risks, Ellie. This isn't your usual bank transaction." The unspoken tension between them, fueled by Ellie's past relationship with Ethan, hung heavy in the air.

"Oh, I'm well aware," Ellie retorted, a hint of defiance in her voice. "After all, I've dealt with far riskier transactions in my career. Some might even say I've had a front-row seat to the inner workings of high-stakes operations." Her gaze lingered pointedly on Ethan, a silent provocation that Ysabel couldn't ignore.

Ysabel felt a surge of anger. but he pressed on, determined to maintain control. She outlined the final details of Operation Medusa, and her military precision was evident in her strategic planning. She spoke of flanking maneuvers, coordinated strikes, and calculated risks, her words sharp and precise. But even her military expertise couldn't mask the growing unease.

As the meeting concluded, Ethan excused himself and promised to pick up his daughter, Lily, from school. Before he left Ysabel's office, he noticed the small book of poetry was not on the desk anymore. Ysabel caught him looking at the space. They looked at each other, wishing either one could say something. But then again, that's for another day.

He left the office, with a tinge of a smile on his face, but his shoulders slumped with exhaustion, his mind weighed down by the investigation and the tension between Ysabel and Ellie.

A chilling phone call later that evening shattered the fragile calm. It was Sergeant Miller, his voice tight with dread. "Mayor Ashworth," he stammered, "there's been an incident... Lily Cole... she's missing."

The blood drained from Ysabel's face. The carefully constructed plans for Operation Medusa, the strategic maneuvers, the calculated risks—all seemed insignificant now, dwarfed by the terrifying reality of Lily's abduction. The celebratory mood of the press conference felt like a distant memory. The city, momentarily relieved, was now plunged back into a chilling darkness. The operation was forgotten. The city was forgotten. All that remained was a desperate race against time, a desperate fight to save a child. The tension had reached a fever pitch, a chilling climax to a day that had begun with hope and ended in despair. The game had changed. And the stakes were infinitely higher.

20

A Frantic Meeting

The mahogany table in Ricardo Alvarez's opulent study gleamed under the harsh glare of the overhead lights. Around it, the key players of Red Stones City's criminal underworld sat, their faces etched with apprehension and excitement. Ricardo, his usual confident demeanor replaced by a nervous energy, paced back and forth, his eyes darting between the assembled figures. Sharneel Kumar, aka Mr. K, sat silently, his imposing figure radiating an aura of controlled power. His face flushed with ambition, Travis Reed fidgeted in his seat, eager to prove his worth. Ever the pragmatist, Wallace Higgins observed the scene with a calculating stillness.

"The Mayor's announcement," Ricardo began, his voice tight with barely controlled anger, "has thrown a wrench into our plans. But it's also given us an opportunity."

He paused, letting his words hang in the air, allowing the tension to build before continuing. "Vince Malone... now that he's decommissioned, we'll not be implicated by it. But now that the video's been exposed, we must proceed with our next move ahead of schedule."

Travis, sensing an opportunity, leaned forward. "I'm ready to take over Vince's operations. I've already recruited and vetted the new team. They're ready to move the goods." His voice was laced with ambition and desperation, a clear attempt to prove his loyalty and capability.

Wallace nodded in agreement. "My trucks are ready. The packages will be distributed throughout the country, and as soon as they arrive, we'll have a new batch of recruits ready to move the goods."

A shadow of concern crossed Mr. K's face. "Ellie Hayes... she's still out there. And she's working with the Mayor's team."

Ricardo waved a dismissive hand. "Ellie is a problem, but a manageable one. We have alternative banks ready for the transactions. I'll split the money laundering into four different times. This way, the new banks won't be alarmed."

Mr. K's gaze remained fixed on Ricardo. "Double the contract on Ellie. One million dollars. Make sure she disappears permanently." The casual brutality of his words sent a chill down the spines of the others.

The meeting continued, a whirlwind of frantic plans and hushed conversations. The deepfake scandal, intended to destabilize the Mayor, had inadvertently accelerated their timeline. The air in the room was thick with a mixture of ambition, fear, and the intoxicating scent of impending danger. Red Stones City was about to experience the full force of their wrath.

Mr. K, his imposing figure radiating an aura of controlled power, suddenly interrupted the chaotic exchange. His voice, usually calm and controlled, now carried a chilling edge. "The Mayor's announcement has created an unforeseen complication," he stated, his gaze sweeping across the faces of his associates. "Ethan Cole's investigation. His persistence is a threat we cannot afford to ignore."

A tense silence settled over the room. Travis Reed, his face pale, shifted uncomfortably in his seat. Wallace Higgins remained impassive. Ricardo Alvarez, however, felt a knot of apprehension tighten in his stomach.

Mr. K's gaze fixed on Ricardo. "Make a call to Detective Inspector Cole," he instructed, his voice low and menacing. "Concisely convey this message: cease his investigation, or he will never see his daughter again."

The casual brutality of the words hung in the air, heavier than the oppressive atmosphere of the room. The implication was chillingly clear: the criminal network was willing to use Lily Cole as leverage to bend Ethan Cole to their will. The frantic energy of the meeting, the rush to capitalize on the unexpected turn of events, was now overshadowed by a cold, calculated cruelty.

Ricardo, his face a mask of conflicting emotions—fear, anger, and determination—nodded curtly. He picked up his phone, his fingers trembling slightly as he dialed the number. The carefully laid plans were now in motion, propelled by the deepfake scandal, but now fueled by a terrifying new element—the abduction of Ethan's daughter. The consequences of their actions were about to be unleashed upon the unsuspecting city, and the personal stakes had just been raised exponentially.

The meeting ended not with a bang but with a chilling, ominous silence, broken only by the ringing of a phone, a sound that echoed the impending doom hanging over Red Stones City. Unseen and unknown to everybody in the room, nestled within the seemingly innocuous pen Travis Reed clutched so dearly, a tiny camera blinked, recording every word, every gesture, every chilling threat. Miles away, Marco Davies witnessed the whole thing.

21

Operation Medusa - Endgame

The grainy image flickered on the big screen in David Davies's room. Several screens displayed various parts of the operation, making it look like the Pentagon's war room. Marco's voice, hushed and urgent, cracked through the headset.

"They're moving up the timeline. Malone's out, but they're already replacing him. They're using Lily as leverage against Cole," came the rapid report of Marco, who was stationed in his special room at the Casino IT department.

"Mr. K... he's terrifying. They're going after Ellie," he continued. "Get this to Ethan immediately."

The live feed from the spy cam embedded in Travis Reed's pen relayed the clandestine meeting in real-time, a crucial piece of intelligence in the escalating battle against Red Stones City's criminal underworld.

Ethan leaned forward; his gaze fixed on the screen. Ysabel, her face grim, sat beside him, her fingers drumming a silent rhythm on the table. "David, get this to Sergeant Miller immediately. He needs to coordinate with the Seal Teams. Marco, keep the feed running as long as possible."

"Roger that," David replied, his fingers flying across the keyboard.

The tension in the room was palpable. The carefully laid plans for Operation Medusa were now in jeopardy. The abduction of Lily had thrown everything into chaos, but this new intel was a lifeline—a chance to strike back.

Outside, the city hummed with its usual nocturnal rhythm, oblivious to the clandestine war unfolding in the Mayor's office. But within those walls, every second felt like an eternity.

Sergeant Miller's voice crackled over the comms: "Seal Team Alpha, reporting in. Ready for deployment."

Ysabel's calm and controlled voice cut through the tension: "Alpha Team, proceed to the designated intercept point. Maintain visual contact with the target plane. Await further instructions."

"Copy that, Mayor," Miller responded.

The minutes ticked by, each one filled with a mixture of hope and dread. The real-time feed showed the frantic activity at the drop point. Two speedboats, their engines roaring, zipped across the dark waters.

"Alpha Team, we have visual confirmation of the drop. Two speedboats approaching the target zone," Miller reported.

Ysabel's eyes narrowed. "Standby. Await my command."

A second plane appeared on the radar. The situation was escalating rapidly.

"Mayor, we have a second target approaching," Miller's voice was urgently tight. "Requesting authorization for immediate engagement."

Ysabel took a deep breath. "Alpha Team, proceed with the pickup. Delta Team, neutralize the speedboats. Charlie and Tango Teams, prepare for the third target. I repeat, Alpha Team, proceed with the pickup."

The comms crackled with the coordinated responses of the various teams. The scene was a whirlwind of activity, a ballet of precision and controlled chaos.

"Alpha Team, packets secured. Moving to rendezvous point."

"Delta Team, speedboats neutralized. Casualties: two confirmed, one apprehended."

"Charlie Team, packets secured. Moving to rendezvous point."

"Tango Team, engaging the hostile target. Requesting backup."

A moment of silence hung in the air, broken only by the rhythmic tapping of Ysabel's fingers on the table. Then, a final report: "Tango Team, hostile targets neutralized. Casualties: four confirmed."

The tension in the room began to ease. The operation was proceeding according to plan.

The final reports came in. Bravo Team had secured the distribution yard, and all the recruits were apprehended without resistance.

Ysabel leaned back, a faint smile playing on her lips. "Operation Medusa is a success. Sergeant Miller, report to the war room. We need to consolidate our intelligence and begin the next phase."

In Ethan's office, the atmosphere was lighter. Marco and David exchanged relieved glances.

At the Mayor's war room, Ysabel was trying to contact Ethan. "Echo, this is Yankee, what's your 20?"

The radio cracked, and Ysabel heard Ethan say, "The pit is quiet, but we see targets moving."

"Do you have a visual for Lima?" Ysabel inquired.

"Negative," was the quick reply.

At Ethan's office, David congratulated the team. "Well done, guys," To the screen, he addressed Marco, "You saved the day, buddy. I am proud of you."

The city slept, unaware of the silent victory that had been won under the cover of darkness. But for those in the know, the night had brought a sense of triumph – a hard-won victory in a war far from over. The battle for Red Stones City had entered a new phase.

22

A House Divided

The opulent study of Ricardo Alvarez was a stark contrast to the turmoil brewing within its walls. Ricardo, his face etched with a mixture of anger and apprehension, paced before Mr. K, who sat rigidly in his chair, his usual calm demeanor replaced by a simmering fury.

"This was a mistake," Ricardo spat, his voice laced with barely controlled rage. "Abducting the Inspector's daughter was reckless. I warned you."

Mr. K's eyes narrowed. "The girl is insurance, Ricardo. A bait to lure Cole. Without her, we have no leverage."

Their argument was interrupted by a frantic knock. Wally Higgins stumbled into the room, his face pale, his breath coming in ragged gasps. "They got them all, Mr. K! Every single one! The trucks... the drivers... even the manager... he's dead!"

Mr. K's controlled fury intensified. He waved a dismissive hand, trying to maintain an air of composure. "Calm yourself, Higgins. We have contingencies."

Before he could finish, Travis Reed burst in, his face equally grim. "The hotel... it was raided. All the recruits are captured. There are no casualties, but they're all under investigation. They know."

The Vice Mayor seized the opportunity. "See, Mr. K? Your reckless actions have jeopardized everything! We need to regroup, reassess, and—"

Mr. K cut him off, his voice dangerously low. "My accounts... they're empty. Every single one." His eyes flashed with a cold fury that sent a chill down Ricardo's spine. He slammed his fist on the desk, the sound echoing in the tense silence that followed. "Bring Lily in. Now."

The command hung in the air, heavy and ominous. The disagreement, failures, and sudden loss of funds culminated in a desperate, reckless decision. Lily, who was meant to be a tool, had become their last resort. The tension in the room was so thick you could cut it with a knife. The stage was set for the rescue attempt, the stakes higher than ever.

The celebratory mood in the Mayor's office was shattered. The news of Ellie's murder hit Ysabel like a physical blow. She stared at Sergeant Miller, her face pale, her eyes wide with disbelief and grief. "Ellie... they killed her," she whispered, her voice barely audible.

Before Miller could respond, Ethan burst into the room, his face grim, his eyes burning with fury. He had just received the devastating news from his surveillance team—the Vice Mayor's house had been compromised, the raid had failed, and Lily was gone.

"They have Lily," Ethan said, his voice raw with emotion. His fury was a palpable force in the room, threatening to consume him.

Just then, a video file arrived, its subject line a chillingly simple: "Insurance." Ysabel and Ethan exchanged a look, a silent acknowledgment of the impending horror. They clicked play.

The grainy image showed Lily, her face pale and tear-streaked, her mouth gagged with duct tape, her clothes torn. Her eyes, wide with terror, darted around the room. She was bound to a chair, her body trembling.

A distorted voice, heavily processed through a voice changer, filled the room. "If you want to keep your daughter alive, follow the instructions that I will send you, and she will live."

The voice, though disguised, held a chilling familiarity. Ysabel, her military training kicking in, recognized the subtle nuances of the syntax. "It's Asian," she said, her voice low and grim. "Filipino or Malaysian, perhaps."

The video ended, leaving a void of terror and helplessness in its wake. The carefully constructed plans, the successful operation—all seemed insignificant now, dwarfed by the terrifying reality of Lily's abduction. The city, momentarily relieved, was now plunged back into a chilling darkness. The game had changed, and the stakes were infinitely higher.

23

The Price of Rescue

The air in the Mayor's office was thick with tension, starkly contrasting to the earlier celebratory mood. The news of Ellie's death hung heavy, a chilling reminder of the risks involved. Ysabel, her face etched with grief and determination, addressed the assembled team.

"We need to rescue Lily," she stated, her voice firm despite the tremor in her hands. "But the question is... how?"

The discussion immediately turned to Ethan's involvement. His close connection to Lily was a double-edged sword. His determination was undeniable, but his emotions might cloud his judgment.

"Ethan, I understand your desire to be involved," Ysabel began, her gaze softening slightly. "But your decisions might be compromised. We lost Ellie. I can't risk losing another member of this team."

Ethan, his face grim, met her gaze. The news of Ellie's death had hit him hard. He hadn't even processed it. He was shocked into silence. Now, all he felt was a burning resolve. "I have to be there, Ysabel. I know the risks, but I can handle it. I'll follow protocol. I promise."

Sergeant Miller, a seasoned veteran who had served alongside Ethan on countless missions, spoke up. "Mayor, with all due respect, Ethan's the best we've got. He's dependable and resourceful, and he knows how to handle high-pressure situations. He'll follow orders. I'll be there to keep him in check."

Ysabel considered their words, her gaze shifting between Ethan and Miller. The weight of her decision was immense. The loss of Ellie was still fresh, a gaping wound in their team. But she knew, deep down, that Ethan was right. His presence was essential.

"Very well," she conceded, her voice heavy with the burden of her decision. "Ethan, you're in. But Sergeant Miller will take point. You will follow the protocol in the letter. No exceptions."

Ethan nodded curtly, his resolve unwavering. Their unspoken understanding was a silent promise: they would do everything in their power to bring Lily home safely.

A few minutes later, a chilling text message arrived. The demands were stark: a fully fueled helicopter ready for immediate deployment and one hundred million dollars in bearer bonds delivered within three hours.

Ysabel's face hardened. "Three hours?" she muttered, her eyes flashing with anger. "They think they can dictate our terms?"

The reply was swift and brutal: "Three hours or parts of Lily will be delivered every ten minutes."

Ysabel, Ethan, and Miller exchanged a look. There was no time for hesitation. They began drafting a rescue plan, with each move calculated and decision carefully weighed. The clock was ticking, and the rescue price was far higher than they had ever imagined.

24

Desperate Measures

The clock ticked relentlessly, each second a hammer blow against the fragile hope of rescuing Lily. Ysabel, Ethan, and Sergeant Miller huddled around a table in the makeshift war room, the tension palpable. The rescue plan, born out of desperation and necessity, was audacious, three-pronged, and inherently risky.

"The chopper delivery is straightforward," Sergeant Miller explained, his voice low and steady. "We'll land it at the helipad. Mr. K's pilot will replace ours, and our pilot will be released unharmed. The bonds will be, in two cases, fifty million each."

"But how do we know they'll release our pilot?" Ysabel sked; her brow furrowed with concern. "And how do we confirm Lily's inside?"

Ethan nodded in agreement. "And what about other people in the house? Guards, reinforcements... we need to account for that."

Miller acknowledged their concerns. "The plan is fluid, yes. It could go wrong at any stage. But changing it now risks Lily's life. They've already shown they're willing to kill."

The weight of their decision hung heavy in the air. The risks were immense, and the stakes impossibly high. Yet, they had no other choice. Thirty minutes later, a revised plan was hatched, a delicate dance of calculated risks and desperate measures.

Sergeant Miller would lead the assault team, a crack unit of highly trained officers. Their objective was swift and precise: neutralize any guards, secure Lily, and extract her without causing any unnecessary casualties. Despite Ysabel's reservations, Ethan would be part of the assault team, and his intimate knowledge of the Vice Mayor's house proved invaluable. A secondary team would secure the perimeter, ensuring no one could interfere with the extraction.

The helicopter would land as planned, and the pilots would be exchanged swiftly. The bonds would be delivered, and Mr. K and the Vice Mayor would be given safe passage to the helicopter. Once airborne, the assault team would move in, utilizing their knowledge of the house layout to minimize the risk to Lily.

A small drone with thermal imaging would be deployed beforehand to confirm Lily's presence and account for potential reinforcements. It would scan the interior of the house, identifying any heat signatures, confirming Lily's location, and providing real-time intelligence to the assault team.

The plan was far from perfect, riddled with potential points of failure. But it was their best chance. The weight of responsibility rested heavily on their shoulders, the fate of Lily hanging precariously in the balance. The countdown had begun.

25

Extraction

The helicopter's rotors sliced through the air, the thrum of the blades a steady reminder of the mission ahead. Sergeant Miller stood at the helm in the makeshift war room, issuing final instructions to the team. Ethan's heart raced as he checked his gear, his thoughts consumed by the urgency of the moment.

"Listen up," Miller said, his voice steady despite the tension in the air. "This is a three-pronged operation. We land the chopper, exchange pilots, and secure Lily. We're moving fast and precise. No mistakes."

The plan was set in motion. As the helicopter descended toward the Vice Mayor's mansion, Ethan's mind raced. They would deliver the bearer bonds as instructed.

The helicopter landed smoothly on the helipad. The team watched as Mr. K's pilot approached, the tension thick in the air. The pilot stepped out, curtly saying, "It's green." Mr. K and the Vice Mayor began to advance, their expressions mixing arrogance and anticipation.

But they didn't know that Ethan had positioned himself behind the pilot's seat, ready to take control. As the pilot was about to confirm the bearer bonds, a gun was pressed against his temple. "Confirm the bonds," Ethan demanded, his voice low and threatening.

The pilot nodded, fear flashing in his eyes. Before he could utter another word, Ethan injected him with a sedative, disabling him instantly. He secured the pilot to the co-pilot's seat to ensure they wouldn't be discovered too soon.

As Mr. K and the Vice Mayor climbed aboard, they were greeted by a shocking sight: Ethan, posing as the pilot, gun drawn. "Welcome aboard," he said with a steely gaze.

The Vice Mayor's eyes widened in horror as he attempted to retreat, but Ethan was quicker. A shot rang out, and the Vice Mayor crumpled to the floor, his body lifeless.

Mr. K, panic etched across his face, clutched the two attache cases filled with bonds. "Wait!" he shouted, desperation creeping into his voice. "I can give you one case! Just let me go!"

"No deal," Ethan replied, his grip tightening on the weapon. "We wait until I get confirmation that my daughter is safe."

Meanwhile, Sergeant Miller's team had breached the house inside the mansion without a hitch. They found Lily quickly, but Wally and Travis attempted to intervene, only to be swiftly disarmed and cuffed. The sound of gunfire echoed as the guards opened fire on the team. A quick exchange ensued, and the four guards were dispatched with practiced efficiency.

"Lily is safe," Miller confirmed over the radio, relief flooding through Ethan at the words. But Mr. K, sensing the tide turning, made a break for it, attempting to flee the chopper.

Before he could escape, a shot rang out, hitting him in the legs. He crumpled onto the helipad, gasping in pain as the team quickly moved to subdue him.

Ethan, unable to contain himself, rushed back toward the house. Lily sat in the dim light of the room, her wide eyes filled with fear and confusion. He scooped her into his arms, holding her as tightly as he could, overwhelmed with relief. "I've got you, sweetheart. You're safe now."

The operation had been swift and efficient, a testament to Sergeant Miller's careful planning and invaluable suggestions. As they exited the house, the weight of the night began to lift. They had succeeded. They had brought Lily home.

26

Sunsets and Shadows

The city, still reeling from the previous night's events, seemed to hold its breath as the sun dipped below the horizon, painting the sky in fiery orange and soft lavender hues. Ethan and Ysabel sat on the beach, a quiet intimacy settling between them, a stark contrast to the recent chaos. Lily was with her grandmother for the night. The breathtaking sunset provided a backdrop for a conversation that had been long overdue.

The air was filled with the gentle sounds of the waves, a soothing balm to their frayed nerves. They spoke of the rescue, of Ellie's loss, of the lingering fear that still clung to them like a shadow. But as the darkness deepened, so did their connection. Their words became less about the past few days' events and more about the feelings that had simmered beneath the surface for so long.

A gentle breeze rustled through the palm trees, carrying the scent of salt and sea. Their eyes met, and a silent understanding passed between them in that shared gaze. Words became unnecessary; their emotions were laid bare in the unspoken language of their hearts.

Ethan reached across the table with a soft sigh, his fingers brushing against Ysabel's. She leaned into his touch, her hand resting warmly in his. Their eyes locked once more, silently acknowledging the unspoken feelings that had bound them together through the trials and tribulations of the past few weeks.

A few whispered words were exchanged, soft as the ocean breeze. Promises, hopes, and dreams for a future together. Then, a kiss. Tentative at first, hesitant, as if testing the waters of a newfound emotion. Then, a deeper, more passionate kiss, a release of pent-up feelings, a culmination of shared experiences and unspoken desires.

As if sensing their intimacy, the sun began to sink below the horizon, casting long shadows enveloping them in a cloak of privacy. It was as if nature itself was conspiring to grant them a moment of seclusion, a sanctuary from the world's harsh realities.

Their embrace deepened, their bodies melting in a silent symphony of love and longing. The world around them faded, leaving only the intensity of their connection.

Suddenly, a small voice broke through their reverie. Lily stood at the edge of the beach, her eyes wide with curiosity, her innocent question hanging in the air. Ysabel and Ethan separated, their faces flushed, their hearts pounding. The moment of intense intimacy was shattered, replaced by a mixture of embarrassment and amusement. The sunset, their witness, seemed to blush a deeper shade of crimson.

"Are you my next mommy?" and Lily rushed to embrace Ysabel, and winked at her dad.

27

New Dawn

Once shrouded in shadows, the city of Red Stones began to bask in the warmth of a new dawn. Ysabel Ashworth, her face etched with quiet confidence, stood on the steps of City Hall, addressing a cheering crowd. Her victory in the mayoral election was a resounding affirmation of the city's resilience, its unwavering hope for a brighter future. The scars of the past few weeks were still visible, but the city was healing, its spirit unbroken.

Meanwhile, Marco and David, their partnership forged in the crucible of the recent crisis, launched their cybersecurity firm. Their expertise in technology and investigation proved invaluable in a world increasingly reliant on digital infrastructure. Their success was a testament to their collaboration and a symbol of the positive changes that were sweeping through Red Stones.

Ethan and Ysabel, their love deepened by the shared trials they had overcome, found a new rhythm in their lives. The playful banter between Ethan and Lily was a constant source of amusement. The warmth of their family life starkly contrasted to the darkness they had recently faced. Their future, though uncertain, was filled with promise, a testament to the resilience of the human spirit.

The setting sun cast long shadows across the city, but darkness no longer held the same power. Red Stones City had faced its demons and emerged stronger, its people united by their shared experiences and collective determination to build a better tomorrow. The future was unwritten, but the city, under Ysabel's steady leadership, was ready to embrace it.

THE END

List of Characters

Main Characters:

- Ysabel Ashworth: Mayor of Red Stones City, formerly in the US military.
- Ethan Cole: Detective Inspector, Ysabel's potential romantic interest. Father of Lily.
- Liam: Ysabel's deceased fiancé, died in a rescue mission.
- Lily: Ethan's daughter.

Antagonists:

- Ricardo Alvarez: Vice Mayor, mastermind of the criminal network.
- Vince Malone: Casino Owner, involved in money laundering and smuggling.
- Sharneel Kumar, aka Mr. K: The mysterious "Man in the Shadows," a high-level figure in the criminal network.
- Ellie Hayes: Bank General Manager, Ethan's childhood girlfriend and Ysabel's university roommate. Involved in money laundering.
- Wallace "Wally" Higgins: Entrepreneur Extraordinaire, owner of Quickducks Moving Company
- Ravis Reed: replaced Vince Malone as Casino Head

Supporting Characters:

- Sergeant Miller: Seasoned detective on Ethan's team.
- Officer Diaz: Tech specialist on Ethan's team.
- Dr. Ramirez: Forensic specialist on Ethan's team.
- Sarah Chen: PR expert on Ethan's team.
- David Davies: Ethan's IT guy, Provides technical support to Ethan.
- Marco Davies: Vince Malone's IT specialist, creates the deepfake video.
- Travis Reed: Head of Operations for Vince Malone in the Casino.
- Trish Evans: Secretary to the Mayor
- Maria, the homeless woman
- Various Informants: People who provide information to Sergeant Miller.

THE PARK CHRONICLES

THE PARK CHRONICLES
a Collection of Short Stories
by Danny Niñal

I DIED THEREFORE I AM
by Danny Niñal

The park was at its most enchanting during twilight. The crepuscular rays radiated from where the sun partially hid behind the trees, casting a warm glow that transformed the leaves from vibrant green to soft shades of yellow, orange, and red.

"Look!" Strauss exclaimed, his voice full of excitement.

"Wow, sir, it's the most beautiful thing I've ever seen!" Bob replied, his eyes wide with wonder, reminiscent of an eight-year-old girl gazing at her favorite Rilakkuma.

"Just wait until the sun sets right behind Trish's top branch," Strauss teased.

"Trish? Who's Trish, sir?" Bob asked curiosity piqued.

"That tall and beautiful tree right in front of me. She's Trish," Strauss replied, as if introducing a girlfriend to his parents.

"I h-h-h-heard that! You're t-t-t-talking about my b-b-b-butt again, Strauss!" Trish interjected playfully.

"Hi, Trish! Meet our new FB (friend-bench), Bob. He was installed this morning—no ribbon-cutting for him, though, like I had," Strauss announced.

"And I've already been peed on by a dog! Hello, Ma'am, nice meeting you!" Bob's laughter echoed through the park.

Trish took a moment, carefully choosing her words for the newcomer. "Nice to m-m-m-meet you too, Bob," she said, a hint of familiarity sparking in her thoughts about this new friend.

"Sir Strauss, why do trees grow so tall and still stand?" Bob asked, gazing up at Trish's towering form, illuminated by the orange clouds behind her.

"The answer isn't up there, young one. It's down below. You're looking at the right page number but in the wrong book," Strauss replied.

"What do you mean, sir?" Bob asked, glancing around as he took in his new surroundings.

"Form follows function," Strauss said, his voice rich with knowledge.

"You're too intelligent for me, sir," Bob admitted, a hint of embarrassment creeping into his words.

"The roots, my boy, the roots. That's where the answer lies. They gather nutrients from the soil and support the weight of the tree's top growth," Strauss explained, his lecture engaging.

"Some primary roots extend almost as deep as the tree's height," he continued. "And secondary 'feeder' roots often stretch far beyond the tree's drip line—the imaginary line around the tree where water drips off the perimeter of its canopy."

"What you c-c-c-can't see, Bob," Trish said gently, "is that r-r-r-roots of trees are almost always intertwined."

Bob pondered the strength of the bond between trees with intertwined roots, feeling a deep sense of familiarity that eluded him.

"Are your actions, Bob, predicated upon your roots?" Strauss asked, seemingly shifting the topic.

"If you're asking whether I know my roots, sir, I believe I do," Bob replied confidently.

"Do you th-th-th-therefore prefer to b-b-b-be where your roots are? Would you be h-h-h-happy if you're reconnected, um, t-t-t-to your roots?" Trish asked, her voice sincere.

"Yes, to both questions, Ma'am. I would be happy," Bob said earnestly.

"For reasons I cannot explain, can I ask your opinion about cutting trees?" Strauss inquired, curiosity evident in his tone.

"Sir, I think it's not the cutting that's wrong; it's how they're cutting the trees that's the issue," Bob articulated thoughtfully.

"Well done, boy," Strauss thought, pleased with the response.

"You're not as dumb as I thought," declared the wise old bench.

"Inexperienced perhaps, but not dumb, sir," Bob corrected himself, trying to be politically correct.

"I agree," Strauss whispered.

"That I am not dumb, sir?" Bob clarified, almost missing the point.

"That too. But I also strongly believe that if trees are made for something—a bench, maybe—then the only way to create a wooden bench is to cut a tree," Strauss emphasized, ensuring his point was understood.

"I die, therefore I am," Bob said philosophically, surprising Strauss. *I'd better be careful with this one,* Strauss thought.

"Are you guys t-t-t-talking about my b-b-b-butt again?" Trish interrupted her voice light.

Both Strauss and Bob exchanged knowing winks, chuckling.

"Good old oaks that we are, we know a good butt when we see one, hahaha!" Strauss exclaimed.

"Strauss, you d-d-d-dirty old oak! I come from a well-bred f-f-f-family of cedars," Trish retorted, her tone posh, as if emulating a royal princess. "Careful, th-th-th-there are young c-c-c-cedars all around!"

"Sir, can I ask you a question?" Bob whispered, glancing around as if the very trees were eavesdropping.

"We'll be sitting here for the rest of our lives, so we might as well get to know each other well. I feel you, man," Strauss replied, his voice warm.

"I see a trunk cut and some widow-makers—dead branches snapped off not too long ago. What happened to that tree?" Bob asked, his curiosity evident.

"Some story, that was. A long one that you don't want Trish to be reminded of," Strauss answered, his tone soft and almost inaudible.

"We have a lifetime ahead of us, sir. You can start from the beginning," Bob encouraged, his eagerness palpable.

"Three years ago, on a summer morning, when the joggers had just left, and people started passing by with coffee in one hand and newspapers in the other, I still clearly remember those two men in hardhats who stopped right before Trish. They sat down, spread a huge sheet of paper, and began pointing all over the park," Strauss began, his voice low, as if sharing a secret.

Bob listened intently, the tension in the air thickening as Strauss continued. "One stood up, walked over to Trish, and looked around her, pointing at the dead branches surrounding the other trees and then at me, shaking his head vigorously."

Bob remained silent, absorbing every word as Strauss whispered, "The other man looked around, pointed at another spot, and they both assessed the area, nodding their heads."

Strauss raised a hand, signaling Bob to hold his thoughts. "Then the second man walked over to Twiggee, circled her, and pointed right at where you are now."

As he returned to the first man, the guy took out his radio and said something. Strauss continued, "I didn't need to know exactly what they said; I already knew. A few minutes later, more people in hardhats arrived, bringing ropes, chainsaws, and even more hardhats." His voice faltered, and it felt like he was sobbing for a moment.

"In the afternoon, more equipment and more hardhats came. The park was closed to the public, so I couldn't hear anyone talking, but the chainsaw... oh, it was starting to sound terrifying," Strauss said, his tone shifting to one of a horror movie narrator.

"Earlier, I agreed with you that there's nothing inherently wrong with cutting trees; it's the way they do it that's wrong," he added, shifting gears.

"Yes, sir, indeed," Bob interrupted, unable to contain himself. "They should plant new trees before they cut any down."

"Since I believe that the only way for me to exist is for me to die first—like I have to be born again," Strauss mused.

"You sound like a minister, sir, but yes, I agree," Bob replied, nodding thoughtfully.

"I've been here for years and never seen a new tree planted. Not one," Strauss mumbled, his voice heavy with sadness. "Although I see flowers and gardens arranged in strategic places."

"They're beautiful, sir, I must admit," Bob said, attempting to find the silver lining.

"Yes, but we're talking about cutting trees now, and the beauty of flowers will never compensate for the loss of a tree," Strauss said, his tone solemn.

Bob fell silent, deep in thought. He began to look around, an uneasy shiver running down his spine. "Was it a cedar that they cut that day?"

"Yes, in fact, it was a cedar. Why do you ask?"

"Well, sir, I think I saw the trunk. That must be Twiggee," Bob said quietly, his heart heavy.

"Yes," Strauss sobbed softly, unabashed.

His thoughts drifted back to that fateful day when they came to cut Twiggee, the memory forever etched in his heart.

"Strauss, are they c-c-c-cutting me now? Are th-th-th-they felling me now? Please, I d-d-d-don't want to die!" Trish screamed in fear. She was one of the oldest trees in the park, and the management had been felling trees for months.

brum-brum-brum-brum-brrrrrrrrrrrrrrrrrrrrr

"Trish, don't you worry. It's not you. It's not you," assured Strauss, the most intelligent bench in the park. Like Trish, he was also one of the oldest. They had become close friends over the years. After all, when you face the same view every day without the option to relocate, you either grow to hate each other or decide to make the best of it. Trish and Strauss chose the latter.

brum-brum-brum-brum-brrrrrrrrrrrrrrrrrrrrr

"Are you s-s-s-sure, Strauss?" Trish's voice trembled as the chainsaw noise grew louder, sending shivers through her branches. She quaked in fear, her leaves fluttering like lost hope. Inside, she felt as if she were dying.

"Look around you, Trish," Strauss urged, his voice steady. "All the trees near you have dead branches. If you were to fall, those limbs could snap off and fly through the air. They call those widow-makers. The cutters are cautious of them."

Trish fell silent, her fear weighing heavily on her bark.

"So if they cut you, the only logical direction for you to fall is towards me. They wouldn't let you drop right on top of the most intelligent bench in the park," Strauss mused, trying to lighten the mood. "You feel me, Trish?"

Trish couldn't respond, her mind swirling with uncertainty.

"If they wanted to cut you, they'd first clear a working space around your base and prepare an escape path. They'd do a brushing out, clipping off small branches close to the ground," Strauss explained, his tone resembling that of a college professor. "But they aren't doing any of that to you. Understand? So don't worry; they are not felling you. You feel me, Trish?"

brum-brum-brum-brum-brrrrrrrrrrrrrrrrrrrrr

Trish's thoughts were a tangled mess, but she looked down to see people with chainsaws surrounding her friend, Twigee. Panic surged back, and she felt her trembling return.

"T-t-t-t-t-twig g-g-g-g-gee-e-e-e-e-e!" she shouted, her voice breaking with desperation.

"Strauss, they're c-c-c-cutting Twiggee. I'm f-f-f-feeling her roots shaking now," Bob said, his voice trembling with despair.

That day, no crepuscular rays were radiating from the sun, only the blood-colored trunks and timber strewn around where Twiggee once stood.

Strauss noticed the tears welling in Bob's eyes and didn't stop him. He waited patiently, just as he did when people sat on him, crying softly, seeking solace.

After a moment, Trish broke the silence. "Bob, are you c-c-c-crying?"

"I know that was a sad story, Bob," she continued gently, "but I didn't realize it was so tragic that it made you shed tears. Oaks don't cry, man; they just sob."

"Sir, I was treated three years ago," Bob replied, his voice quivering.

"So?" Strauss prompted, sensing the weight behind Bob's words.

"I am a cedar, sir," Bob said, his admission hanging like a heavy fog.

Trish and Strauss exchanged glances, then turned to look at the spot where Twiggee used to stand.

All Strauss could muster was a banal yet heartfelt, "Welcome home, man."

WHAT IS PLEASURE WITHOUT PAIN

PROLOGUE
At the West Entrance of the park, a woman strolled leisurely with her dog—a ten-pound Bichon Frise standing about ten inches tall at the shoulders. Its fluffy, curly coat featured a soft, dense undercoat, while the outer coat was coarser and curlier, predominantly white with a touch of cream around its ears.

The woman was clearly in the home stretch of her pregnancy, likely in her third trimester, expecting her baby at any moment. Yet, despite her condition, she cherished her daily walks in the park, making it a part of her routine. She was an athletic woman, determined to stay active.

As she walked slowly, savoring the sights and sounds of the park, she approached a newly installed bench. Suddenly, she felt a rush of warmth between her legs, instantly soaking the seams of her pants and trickling around her ankles. Panic surged through her, and she quickened her pace toward the bench, squeezing her thighs together as best as she could.

Sensing her distress, her dog jumped onto the bench and cuddled up to her, offering silent comfort. In a moment of serendipity, he nudged her mobile phone from the side pocket of her jogging pants and managed to dial her husband.

"Hun, I think my water just broke," she managed to say, her voice trembling with a mix of excitement and anxiety.

THREE HOURS AGO
Ring ring ring
The classroom erupted into a flurry of activity as students scrambled to gather their belongings. Amidst the pandemonium, the

teacher watched as boys and girls raced toward the door, eager to reach the school gymnasium for the Inter-Department Basketball Finals.

Ring ring ring

By the second bell, everyone had transformed into a sea of team colors, their enthusiasm infectious. Boys and girls shouted slogans, their cheers echoing through the halls. Cheerleaders' skirts—long enough to avoid being mistaken for belts—swirled around the court, much to the boys' delight.

Ring ring ting

The final bell rang, and the classrooms emptied, or nearly so. Everyone had flocked to the gymnasium except for Hugh. Still undecided whether to watch the game or head home, he adjusted his thick eyeglasses, precariously perched on the edge of his nose. The lenses, thick enough to magnify his already large eyes, had made him a target for the school bullies, who had dubbed him "Little Huge." Basketball held no interest for him, and being the smallest boy in class only exacerbated his situation.

Little Huge gathered his bag, deciding to break from his usual routine. Unbeknownst to him, this decision would mark a turning point in his otherwise ordinary life.

As he walked away from the school, the cheers and jeers from the gymnasium faded into the distance. With each step, he felt a sense of liberation, as if unshackling himself from the school bullies. The world seemed to expand around him, welcoming him into its vastness. In this moment of solitude, he sauntered along, lost in thought, almost missing the turn toward the western entrance of the park—a place he had visited just three days earlier with his mother.

The park looked familiar, with its towering trees, vibrant flowers, inviting benches, and meticulously maintained grounds. It was peaceful, except for a few individuals enjoying their activities. Women strolled with their dogs, which paused occasionally to sniff the grass. Flush from an hour of taebo exercises, others continued their workout to the rhythmic beat of music from their iPods. Hugh was grateful for the park's tranquillity; he had at least a few hours to spare.

Then, his visit took an unexpected turn. A sense of excitement, inexplicable and thrilling, washed over him. It all began when he spotted two butterflies—the most exquisite he had ever seen. Their wings displayed colors he never knew existed. Captivated, he didn't realize that more butterflies surrounded him, their movements forming a solemn ritual pattern. Their fluttering wings seemed almost sublime.

Then, Hugh discovered why they were there, and he nearly dropped to his knees.

Meanwhile, in the Animal World

Angie was one of the most beautiful butterflies in the park, if not the most attractive. The male butterflies longed to be near her, while the females aspired to emulate her grace and charm. No butterfly had ever exerted such a profound influence on the kaleidoscope of butterflies in the park.

Angie embodied a curious blend of maturity and the carefree spirit of a preteen butterfly, which she still was. Her frequent bursts of playfulness belied an intelligence that allowed her to engage in discussions that could befuddle butterflies far older than herself. She often facilitated essential discussions concerning their pressing issue: the Interruption and Intervention of Metamorphosis (or the IIM).

The Council of Butterflies in the Park had convened several meetings, conferences, and seminars to address this troubling phenomenon. The urgency of their discussions stemmed from the pain and suffering caused by the tragic fate of Pupa James. He never had the chance to become an adult butterfly because a human had carelessly sliced open his cocoon before the time was right. Without the strength to grow his wings, Pupa James remained trapped in a liminal state, his eyes bulging grotesquely from their sockets, held in place only by the fragile skin around what should have been his head. His suffering was brief; he died three days after being pulled from his cocoon.

On that day, even Angie's beauty was overshadowed by the gloom of their circumstances. They were en route to bury her brother, Little Pupa James. According to the fact-finding committee's report, a human had seen the cocoon, unaware that Pupa James was undergoing metamorphosis inside it. He should have transformed into a fully developed butterfly at this critical stage. James never had the chance to complete this transformation, and the human who intervened had unwittingly sentenced him to death.

James had developed into a larva (or caterpillar) from an egg. By nature's design, he spun a silk-like cocoon around himself. Like all butterflies, James' adult structure would have formed through the secretions of two tiny glands known as "Corpora Allata," which released Juvenile Hormones (JH). These hormones would influence another set of glands called the "Prothoracic glands," which in turn secreted a hormone called Ecdysone. Together, JH and Ecdysone controlled molting, growth, and pupation, leading to the emergence of a vibrant adult butterfly.

Unfortunately, because the cocoon had been split open, the larva did not undergo the necessary hormonal growth and transformation processes. He was born before his time, and his life ended before it could truly begin. Like all butterflies, James needed to endure the pain of molting and growing through pupation. He missed the joy of existing as a beautiful butterfly without this struggle.

Angie referred to this tragic event as the Intervention and Interruption of Metamorphosis. She vowed to dedicate her life to showcasing her beauty and intelligence and preventing IIM from affecting any future larvae in the park.

But for now, Angie and her friends turned their focus toward the solemn task of burying her brother, Little Pupa James.

LITTLE HUGE

The boy was so engrossed in the solemn display before him that he didn't realize he had been watching the event for half an hour. Then, something caught his eye that would forever change his life—the cocoon. It looked familiar, and as he stared, a shiver ran down his spine when he recognized it as the same cocoon he had split open three days earlier. He had done it in a misguided attempt to help, believing the larva inside was suffering from pain. He had only wanted to ease its distress, and he recognized the distinctive cut made by his scissors—lengthwise, right of center.

On top of the cocoon lay the lifeless larva, ceremoniously carried by several ants. Then, butterflies formed two solemn columns, and with the ants' help, the butterflies buried their dead—the very larva Little Huge had killed.

He knelt, not out of reverence for the deceased, but because his knees had weakened under the weight of his realization. Instead of helping the larva, he had ended its life. Guilt washed over him like a tidal wave, and he recalled the words of his art teacher.

"Hugh, I did not create this wooden sculpture. It was already there. I just chipped away the unnecessary pieces," his teacher had explained when classmates praised the exquisite carving of a swan made from a tree trunk in the park.

"It must have been painful for the trunk when you chiseled those parts, sir," Little Huge had imagined, envisioning the trunk as a living swan.

"There are things we only achieve through trials and difficulties in life," the teacher replied. "A friend of mine phrased it much better."

"How did he write it, sir?" Hugh had asked, intrigued.

"He said, 'Rainbows are not made without the millions of droplets of rain, just as happiness is not achieved without enduring lots of pain,'" the teacher recited, his voice filled with reverence as if quoting poetry.

"Then I would say it this way, sir: 'What is pleasure without pain?'" Little Huge proclaimed, spreading his arms dramatically as if he were the lead in a production of *Hamlet*.

"That's another way of saying it. You're quite insightful, my little friend," the sculptor had replied, a proud smile on his face.

Hugh was jolted back to reality when an ant bit him on the right foot, the sharp pain snapping him out of his reverie.

At the West Entrance of the park, a woman strolled leisurely with her dog—a ten-pound Bichon Frise standing about ten inches tall at the shoulders. Its fluffy, curly coat featured a soft, dense undercoat, while the outer coat was coarser and curlier, predominantly white with a touch of cream around its ears.

The woman was clearly in the home stretch of her pregnancy, likely in her third trimester, expecting her baby at any moment. Yet, despite her condition, she cherished her daily walks in the park, making it a part of her routine. She was an athletic woman, determined to stay active.

As she walked slowly, savoring the sights and sounds of the park, she approached a newly installed bench. Suddenly, she felt a rush of warmth between her legs, instantly soaking the seams of her pants and trickling around her ankles. Panic surged through her, and she quickened her pace toward the bench, squeezing her thighs together as best as she could.

Sensing her distress, her dog jumped onto the bench and cuddled up to her, offering silent comfort. In a moment of serendipity, he nudged her mobile phone from the side pocket of her jogging pants and managed to dial her husband.

"Hun, I think my water just broke," she managed to say, her voice trembling with excitement and anxiety.

"Okay. Stay where you are; I'm on my way. I will call an ambulance," the husband replied calmly, his voice betraying none of the anxiety and tumultuous thoughts in his mind. This would be their third baby; finally, it was a boy. Their two daughters were ecstatic, constantly asking when their little brother would arrive.

Meanwhile, the woman anxiously scanned her surroundings for her husband or the approaching ambulance, oblivious to the boy passing by. Little Hugh was so lost in his thoughts that he didn't notice the woman sitting on the bench, although he saw the dog wagging its tail beside her.

Determined to ease his guilt, Little Hugh went to the Park Office and asked to speak with the manager. They discussed various ideas for about an hour until, finally, the manager agreed to his proposal.

"Hugh, the park will become even more beautiful next spring. Thank you for coming and sharing your suggestions," the manager said with a smile.

"I just want to do my part, sir," Little Huge replied earnestly.

"Tomorrow, I'll start the campaign to protect the butterflies and create posters detailing their lifecycle. This will help educate people and prevent the larvae from being interrupted..."

Suddenly, they were interrupted by the piercing wail of an ambulance.

"WEEEEOOO! WEEEEOOO! WEEEEOOO!"

"What's going on?" the manager asked his staff, all staring out the window.

"A woman is giving birth at the park, sir," one of the staff members reported.

Hugh dashed out of the office just as the ambulance sped past him, making its way through the Main Gate.

As he headed toward the park's west entrance, he spotted the two butterflies fluttering gracefully among the rest of the swarm. A smile spread across his face, a feeling of hope and purpose blooming within him.

In that moment, Hugh understood that while life could be filled with pain and guilt, it also held the potential for redemption and beauty.

APPEARANCES

Things are not always as they seem; the first appearance deceives many.
— Phaedrus

Prologue
17:15:56

"George, come on, make that face!" James urged, his voice tinged with excitement.

"What face?" George replied, confusion furrowing his brow.

"That face—the one that makes you look like a priest in front of the tabernacle!" James insisted, practically bouncing with anticipation.

"Come on, James. All mantises know how to look like they're praying," George grumbled, rolling his eyes.

"But nobody does it better than you! You really make them believe you're praying. So please, make that face. Hurry!" James's urgency sent a chill down George's exoskeleton.

With a resigned sigh, George started bobbing his head back and forth, both front legs poised for the act. But doubt crept in, and he whispered, "But why, James? I'm just a mantis."

"Because I see the butt," James replied, his voice now pitched higher with urgency.

"What? Whose butt? Where?" George's eyes widened in alarm.

"That butt!" James pointed emphatically at a man sitting on a new bench in the park.

"That butt again?" George echoed, incredulous.

The two mantises perched right in front of a man whose eyes glistened with unshed tears. His knees shook, and his hands trembled uncontrollably. Dusk had settled over the park, casting long shadows as the sun slipped behind the tall trees. The man didn't notice the beauty of the sunset; he couldn't. His mind was lost, and in more ways than one, so was his soul.

In his right hand, he gripped a black metallic object. James's voice softened, almost reverent. "Yes, the butt of a gun."

At the House
15:01:38

The house was empty, save for the man slumped on the settee in the lounge, facing the ocean. The view was spectacular—an expanse of shimmering blue that typically sparked romance and love, candle-lit dinners, and laughter. But today, for this man cradling a double scotch whiskey in his right hand, the breathtaking scenery only served to amplify the memories of happier days long gone and the profound emptiness that enveloped him.

At that moment, he still couldn't comprehend why his family had left him.

In his left hand, he held a piece of paper his wife had placed on the side table in the bedroom. The words were clearly written, but the last letters were smeared, as if tears had fallen onto the page while she wrote.

"THINGS ARE NOT WHAT THEY SEEM."

He couldn't remember how long ago his family had left or when he had arrived home. His mind was foggy, the memories muddled; he must have passed out on the lounge after the party celebrating his promotion to Vice President for Operations.

"With a beautiful wife, lovely kids, a happy family," one of his colleagues had said, raising a glass in toast. "And now a senior partnership in the company, what more can you ask for?"

"I wish I were like you, man," another colleague chimed in, laughter echoing around him.

He could still hear the whispers as he passed by during the festivities, the compliments that felt like daggers now.

"He has a very happy family," one young manager had remarked.

"You should see his wife and kids," another added. "I wish my wife were as beautiful. And he goes to church every Sunday!"

"Hey buddy, maybe you should start going to church too."

"Is that where the beautiful women are? You've made me a convert, man. Hallelujah!"

The man recalled that it was only after he drank his coffee, the bitter taste lingering on his tongue, that he noticed the note. It hadn't sunk in at first that they had left him for good—until he opened the empty drawers and closets, where his wife and children's belongings used to be.

He had called his parents, her parents, her friends, and even their friends' parents. He had reached out to everyone he could think of. But nobody seemed to know where his family had gone, or perhaps they were just unwilling to tell him.

Desperation clawed at him as he dialed his wife's mobile, only to hear it go straight to voicemail.

Nothing.

His wife still hadn't called him... or would she?

At The Park
15:06:32

About a kilometer away from the man's house lay the park, a vibrant picture of joy. Children laughed and played, elderly Chinese practiced a taebo-like routine, and a group of teenagers performed tricks on their skateboards. Birds chirped merrily, and the trees swayed gracefully in the gentle afternoon breeze.

Even the animals seemed happy.

Strauss, the most intelligent bench in the park, observed the two praying mantises as they scampered around, searching for their next meal. Intrigued by their conversation, he called them over, much like a judge summoning lawyers to the stand.

"Hey, Strauss," the older mantis, James, began, "If I look like a monkey and act like a monkey, am I a monkey?"

"Not necessarily, James," Strauss replied, adopting the authoritative tone of a university professor. "If you look like you're praying, are you truly praying?"

"Not necessarily," George, the younger mantis, chimed in. "But my appearances do not define who I am."

"Exactamente! Bravo! Bravissimo, Giorgio!" Strauss exclaimed, his enthusiasm palpable. He could have stretched his arms like an Italian celebrating, but he wasn't Italian—he hailed from the boreal forests of Canada, one of the few trees cut from that pristine area of the world.

"But let me tell you something about appearances," Strauss continued, his tone taking on a more serious note.

"We better sit down; looks like it's going to be a long one," James said, settling in.

"George," James whispered to his younger brother, his front legs poised in readiness should the situation require it.

"Giorgio, you speak of appearances in relation to your true self," Strauss explained. "Sometimes what is inside is revealed by what is outside. That is the level of transparency, and it differs from each of us. Some people are very good at hiding their true feelings, while others can't conceal them at all."

"Sounds like you're talking about actors and actresses—or maybe politicians," George suggested, a knowing glint in his eye.

"Giorgio, you're too clever to be a mantis. You should be a monkey," Strauss joked, and they all laughed. "But you may be onto something. That's why this world adores actors and actresses—they're skilled at becoming who they are not. If you want more intelligent opinions, talk to the new bench in the park, Bobbie," he said, nodding toward a newly installed bench nearby.

The two mantises bid farewell to Strauss, unaware that they would soon play a crucial role in the unfolding drama.

At The House
17:11:42

Back in the empty house, the man still had no idea where his family was. Darkness crept in, and he felt the weight of isolation pressing down on him.

He made his way to the small bar near the kitchen, pouring himself another scotch. As he poured, his gaze fell upon the flower vase his wife had brought back from France. The flowers looked so real that he could almost smell their sweet fragrance.

Memories flooded back—how beautiful she was, how deeply she had loved him... or had she? Everything felt untrue and surreal, blurring the line between reality and illusion. Was his wife's love as fake as the plastic flowers in the vase?

To the outside world, they were the picture of a happy, successful family—a model Christian family at that. People admired them, inviting them to small groups to speak about their seemingly perfect lives. But why had his wife and children left him? Was she seeing someone else? Had she returned to her old life?

Then, out of the corner of his eye, something caught his attention beneath the maple kitchen island—the spot where his wife loved to sit. It was her favorite part of the house, a place she had chosen specifically to match the kitchen's design.

Beneath the island, a shiny object glimmered in the dim light—it was his wife's mobile phone. It wasn't switched on. She never turned her phone off; it was always with her, filled with selfies and Facebook updates.

With trembling hands, he pulled it out and switched it on. His heart raced as excitement surged within him, only to be quickly overshadowed by a wave of dread when he noticed an unsent message on the screen.

Without hesitating, he dashed outside the house and sprinted all the way to the park.

At the Park
17:13:54

He reached the park just as everyone was leaving. Spotting an empty bench, he made a beeline for it, gasping for breath, sweat dripping down his face as if he had just sprinted a hundred-meter dash. Well, didn't he?

Still trying to catch his breath, he noticed a bag left behind. The park was quiet now, the chill of the evening air contrasting with his perspiration. Curiosity piqued, he approached the bag, and when he peered inside, his heart dropped.

It was a gun.

He held the weapon carefully, the weight familiar, pulling him back to his days as an operative. He didn't want to remember those moments, so he was trembling.

As he grappled with his thoughts, he noticed two praying mantises bobbing their heads as if trying to catch his attention. Their alien-looking eyes stared at him, unblinking.

At the Park
17:15:56

"George, come on, make that face!" James urged, his voice filled with urgency.

"What face?" George replied, confusion knitting his brow.

"That face—the one that makes you look like a priest in front of the tabernacle!"

"Come on, James, all mantises look like they're praying," George grumbled.

"But nobody does it better than you! You really make them believe you're praying. So please, make that face. Hurry!" James's urgency was palpable, sending a shiver down George's exoskeleton.

With a reluctant sigh, George began bobbing his head back and forth, both front legs poised for the act. "But why, James? I'm just a mantis," he whispered, fear creeping in.

"Because I see the butt," James replied, his voice rising with urgency.

"What? Whose butt? Where?"

"That butt!" James pointed at the man sitting on the new bench.

"That butt again?" George echoed, disbelief coloring his tone.

They were now right in front of a man whose eyes glistened with tears, knees shaking, hands trembling. The sun was dipping below the tall trees, casting long shadows across the ground. The man didn't notice the beauty of the sunset; he couldn't. His mind was lost, and in more ways than one, so was his soul.

In his right hand, he held the black metallic object.

"Yes, the butt of a gun," James said, his gaze fixed on the man. "I've seen those eyes before. A man shot himself right in front of me. I don't want to witness that again, George."

"Do you want us to look like we're begging him not to shoot himself? What if he turns the gun on us instead? Hello?" George retorted, anxiety creeping into his voice.

The man stared at the mantises, momentarily forgetting his dire situation. They were oddly entertaining, and in that moment of distraction, he realized something profound—he had forgotten to pray.

He hadn't prayed to God to keep his family safe. He hadn't even thought to ask anyone to pray for them. All that consumed his mind were his own worries and helplessness.

Looking up, he saw the tall tree in front of him, sunlight filtering through its branches, creating a heavenly glow. The sight was magnificent, and he wept.

Then he heard it—a sound, faint at first but unmistakable.

At the Park
17:24:16
"Daaaddy-y-y-y-y-y!"

As he turned toward the voice, he saw his wife and two daughters running toward him. Without hesitation, he jumped up and rushed to them, nearly crushing the two mantises in front of him. He hugged his daughters tightly, feeling a surge of love wash over him that he had almost forgotten.

"Are you all right, guys?" he asked, his voice thick with emotion.

He turned to his wife, kissing her with such urgency and passion that it felt like he was a young boy stealing his first kiss. She looked at him, then at the gun in his hand, concern etched across her face.

"Looks like you haven't slept in days, hun," she whispered, wrapping her arms around him.

"I haven't. And this gun isn't mine. Are you okay, hun?"

"Daddy, Daddy! You should've seen Mommy kick those bad guys! They never saw it coming!" his youngest daughter exclaimed, her hands poised like a little karate kid.

"Yes, Dad, Mom was amazing! She kept us safe. I never knew she could move like a ninja. She made the kidnappers think they were in control, but I knew Mom was in charge all along!" his older daughter chimed in, pride shining in her eyes.

"Well, I just waited for the right moment, and they made a mistake," his wife replied, a hint of triumph in her voice.

"They messed with the wrong woman," he joked, trying to lighten the mood. "But you failed to send the message."

"I hid it under the kitchen table in a hurry, but obviously, you got the message. We always meet here at dusk, like those bees in summer," she winked at him.

"I knew they were amateurs," she continued. "When I told them to empty my closets and drawers to make it look like we'd left you, they smiled and said, 'Good thinking.' I somehow knew they would make a mistake along the way. And they did. They untied me so I could punch in the password and transfer the money online. It was all I needed to kick their butts— all three of them!"

"Well, I told you your mom was British," he said, pride swelling in his chest.

"Yes, Dad, but you didn't tell us she was with MI6!" his daughter added with wide eyes.

The man glanced at his wife and winked, and they all erupted into laughter.

"Let's go home," he said, his voice cracking with relief and joy.

Meanwhile, James and George exchanged glances, their hearts swelling with happiness as they realized they had prevented a man from taking his own life.

"James, were you really praying?" George asked, a touch of curiosity in his voice.

"No, were you?" James replied, tilting his head.

"Yes, I was really praying that I would act like I'm praying," George confessed, a grin spreading across his face.

"I always wanted to be an actor," James said, and they both chuckled at the absurdity of the moment.

And so it was.

LOVE: A MONKEY'S BUSINESS

PROLOGUE
A persistent yet polite knock echoed through the tree house. Lovelyn, her heart thrumming with excitement, rushed to the door, its frame newly reinforced with fragrant twigs. Her carefully rehearsed introductions faltered.

"Good evening. This is my father, China, and my mother, Gino," she began, her parents exchanging amused glances. "I mean... Father Gino, Mother China. Oh, sorry... Please meet my parents, China and Gino." Blushing furiously, she gestured towards them.

China, ever the poised matriarch, smoothly took over. Offering her hand with regal grace, she greeted their visitors. "Hello, I'm China, the mother."

"And I'm Gino, the father. Welcome," he added, his smile lingering a beat longer on the mother of the visiting pair. Their eyes met, a silent connection sparking between them, a feeling Gino hadn't experienced in years.

The visitors chorused a greeting, their voices surprisingly harmonious.

The evening progressed smoothly. Lovelyn and her boyfriend, despite their obvious affection, maintained a decorous distance—until a fleeting touch of fingers as they retrieved leaf plates shattered their restraint. He pulled her close, whispering, "Oh, my lovely Lovelyn," before inadvertently dropping a plate. *(The ensuing events are omitted to maintain a GP rating.)*

Dinner was a lavish affair: China's Banana Pie with caramelized, honey-glazed bugs, served on a green leaf with crushed berries, followed by a dessert of one-day-old insects wrapped in a young leaf. (Insects, of course, were a Capuchin monkey culinary staple.)

China noticed something familiar about the boyfriend's father during dessert – a shared recognition mirrored in his fleeting glance. The electric tension between them was undeniable, culminating in a simultaneous gaze at each other's right hands. Then, both collapsed, unconscious. Both were missing their index fingers.

TWELVE YEARS AGO

THE DEAD MONKEY

As twilight descended, the park grew quieter, the chorus of crickets intensifying to announce the imminent arrival of night. Suddenly, the stillness shattered with a piercing scream akin to a relentless fire alarm. A young boy raced into his father's arms, sobbing uncontrollably, his finger pointing toward the freshly cut stump of a tree.

The father hurried to the spot, dread building in his chest. What he found sent a chill through the onlookers: a lifeless capuchin monkey sprawled behind the stump, partially hidden beneath fallen branches. Its blank eyes stared into the eerily serene void as if lost in a meditative trance.

Looking up, the father spotted a monkey perched high in the tree. Sadness radiated from the primate's gaze, and he could almost feel its grief.

THE MONKEY LEADERSHIP

Half a mile away, five elderly capuchin monkeys convened in a serious meeting. Each leader commanded a troop of 10 to 20 monkeys, but Tubby, known as the Capo di Tutti Capi—the Godfather—was acknowledged as the Leader of Leaders. Dominant yet wise, Tubby was revered for his fair and just decisions. Capuchin monkeys were known for their intelligence, but Tubby's experiences set him apart; he had traveled widely, gaining insights unmatched by any other monkey in the park.

The dead monkey was Tubby's eldest son.

"It can only be Spikes," one leader asserted, and the others nodded in grim agreement. Spikes had been expelled from their ranks for proposing the owl monkeys' practice of monogamy, a notion abhorred by the troops. Rumors swirled that Spikes was a half-breed, sired by an owl monkey, and though some monkeys privately agreed with him, they kept silent to preserve their mating privileges, especially since the leader had "primary rights."

"Why would Spikes harm one of his few followers?" the youngest leader questioned, confusion evident in his voice.

"Maybe Tubby's son took Spikes' mate. Who knows? These things happen," another whispered, careful to avoid Tubby's ears.

"That's exactly why I oppose monogamy. It breeds conflict and disharmony within troops. Why should we abandon traditions handed down by our ancestors?" Haig, the eldest, launched into his habitual lecture, preparing for a lengthy soliloquy.

Tubby remained unnervingly silent, his gaze unfocused. When he finally spoke, the room fell silent.

"I want a full investigation immediately. Haig, you will lead this effort and report to me every three hours until the trial is prepared. All suspects must be given their rights to defend themselves. You have five days," Tubby commanded, his authority palpable. No one dared question his orders. One by one, the leaders departed Tubby's tree-house.

Haig was the last to leave. Was there a hint of a smile on his face? Tubby dismissed the thought and redirected his focus to the pressing matter: Spikes.

THE EXPELLED MONKEY

Perched high in the tree, Spikes watched the frantic scene unfold below. The man who rushed to Tubby's son's lifeless body glanced up at him, then back to the deceased monkey, his expression shifting as if he were drawing conclusions about Spikes's involvement in the tragedy. If only they knew the truth.

Spikes's prehensile tail tightened around the branch as he fought back tears. His body trembled with a mixture of grief and rage, each spasm causing the tree to sway ominously.

"How can something so beautiful lead to such a devastating consequence?" he wondered. The idea of finding a single mate and raising offspring together made perfect sense to Spikes, just as it had for Tubby's eldest son, Dave.

Dave and his wife were a beacon of loyalty among the troops, often celebrated for their unwavering commitment. Their bond was a model for others—filled with love and companionship—and they frequently spoke about fidelity and devotion at gatherings. Under Spikes's leadership, his troop flourished, growing in both numbers and reputation. What made them particularly enviable was the unity among their members.

Yet many loathed Spikes, and none more than Haig. The elder had lost several female members to Spikes's troop, blaming him for his own decline. Even those who remained began to embrace monogamy, including Haig's son, Gino, who openly defied his father. "You oppose Spikes simply because you fear losing your right to mate," Gino had argued, igniting tensions within the troop.

The wail of sirens jolted Spikes back to reality. Below, the man called for help as others carefully carried away the dead body of Tubby's son. Overwhelmed, Spikes finally let the tears flow. Why did this have to happen? The vision of a united troop had seemed within reach; their approach had worked.

The only dark cloud that loomed over Spikes's troop was the threat of expulsion—when a "single" monkey became aggressive, attacking a couple in a bid to usurp the male partner, leading to the expulsion of the original male, whether voluntarily or otherwise. Such incidents were rare, but their impact was profound.

Yet Tubby's son hadn't been booted out; someone had made it look that way. Spikes's gaze hardened as he recalled the scene beside the dead body. He knew in his heart that the truth was more sinister than mere expulsion; someone had killed him.

THE MONKEY'S REPORT

Five weeks later, Haig stood before the assembly, ready to present his findings.

"It is with a heavy heart that I present the results of our investigation," he began, his tone signaling the start of what promised to be a lengthy and tedious discourse.

"Oh, please. Wake me up when he's done," one leader muttered, stifling a yawn.

"Kick my knee if I snore, okay?" the other leader whispered back, chuckling quietly.

After nearly an hour of detailed facts and evidence, Haig concluded, "It's an open-and-shut case. Dave committed suicide after being expelled." He then launched into his familiar tirade against monogamy, linking it to the dangers of expulsion, depression, and now, suicide.

"Why did he cut his index finger?" Tubby interjected, his voice piercing through Haig's rhetoric.

"We can only speculate on that matter, Tubby," Haig replied, adjusting his stance. "However, we have sources indicating that among the owl monkeys—whose ludicrous idea of monogamy Spikes adopted..." He slammed his fist on the table for emphasis.

"Stick to the issue, Haig, and save your comments on monogamy unless absolutely necessary," Tubby warned, his tone firm. The murmurs among the leaders grew quieter as they refocused.

"Yes, Tubby. As I was saying, among the owl monkeys, couples whose partner is expelled participate in a Japanese-like ceremony, cutting their index fingers as a symbol of their love for one another," Haig explained.

He concluded his report, leaving a heavy silence in the room. They believed the case was closed, but uncertainty lingered like a shadow in the air.

TEN YEARS LATER

LOVE: THE MONKEY'S BUSINESS

Over the next ten years, Spikes and his troop flourished, demonstrating to the other groups that the practice of monogamy was beneficial for couples and the troop as a whole. Intermarriages among troops became common, and Tubby decreed that if a female capuchin chose a mate from Spikes's troop, no other male could mate with her; violations would result in expulsion from the park and relocation to the zoo. The same rule applied to any male who took a partner from Spikes's troop—he would lose his mating rights across all forces.

But on this particular evening, Spikes's mind was elsewhere. He was focused on calming his grandson, Leo, who was nervously preparing to meet his girlfriend's family for the first time.

"Don't worry, kid. Your parents will be with you. If you're unsure about something, just ask your dad; he's very smart," Spikes reassured him, referring to Ramonito, the partner of Spikes's most beautiful daughter.

"What's your girlfriend's name again, Lovely?" Spikes asked.

"No, Grandpa, it's Lovelyn—with an 'N' at the end," Leo corrected him, rolling his eyes.

"Ah, lovely Lovelyn without end!" They both chuckled. "I'm sure she's as beautiful as your mother," Spikes added, nudging Leo playfully.

"Knock, knock, knock."

The sound echoed through their tree house, prompting everyone to find their places. The knocking was persistent yet not intrusive. "It must be them!" Lovelyn exclaimed, her excitement palpable as she walked toward the door.

She opened the door, which was adorned with fresh twigs added that morning by her father. The fragrant scent of the twigs did little to calm her nerves. Lovelyn began the introductions while trying to steady her trembling limbs, recalling her mother's instructions while maintaining her radiant smile.

"Good evening, this is my father, China, and my mother, Gino," she said, eliciting quizzical looks from her parents.

"I mean, Father Gina and Mother Chino. Oh, I'm sorry! Please meet my parents, China and Gino." Lovelyn blushed deeply.

Like any caring mother, China stepped in gracefully, extending her right limb for a gentle shake. "Hello, I'm China, the mother."

"And I'm Gino, the father. Welcome!" he smiled warmly, lingering a moment longer on the mother of the visiting pair. Their eyes met briefly, a spark of recognition flashing between them—something Gino hadn't felt in a long time.

"Hello!" the visitors chimed together, their voices harmonizing like a choir singing Handel's Hallelujah.

The evening unfolded smoothly. Lovelyn and her boyfriend managed to navigate the night without a hint of romance, although their fingers grazed as they retrieved leaf plates from the tree kitchen. Unable to resist, he pulled her into a warm embrace. "Oh, my lovely Lovelyn," he whispered in her ear, causing a leaf plate to clatter to the ground. *(The ensuing moments were omitted to maintain a GP rating.)*

Dinner was a culinary delight, with China's Banana Pie featuring caramelized bugs drizzled with honey, served on a green leaf and garnished with crushed berries. For dessert, they savored one-day-old insects wrapped in a young green leaf—after all, no meal was complete for capuchin monkeys without insects.

After dinner, China noticed something familiar about the boyfriend's father. Their eyes met, and an electric charge filled the air, palpable and undeniable. In a synchronized moment, they both glanced at each other's right limbs.

Then, as if struck by a force beyond their control, they collapsed to the floor, unconscious. Both were missing their index fingers.

"Where am I?" China mumbled, her surroundings blurry. "Where is Dave?"

"Calm down, China. Just rest. You and Ramonito collapsed," Gino said, trying to comfort her, hesitant to ask who Dave was.

"Sheena! Sheena! Where are you? What happened?" China's voice trembled with confusion.

"Don't stand up, Dad. Just lie down, please. You collapsed," Leo urged softly, seeking to calm his father.

"What's going on? Who's Dave? Who's Sheena?" Gino questioned, bewildered.

THE REAL MONKEY

"They're Dave and Sheena," Spikes declared, pointing at the two still sprawled on the floor.

"China's name used to be Sheena, and Ramonito's real name is Dave," he explained, his tone authoritative, like a pope declaring doctrine. "Ten years ago, they were partners. Back then, the troops didn't accept the idea of having one mate. Someone went to great lengths to prove that it was wrong, hoping to prevent it from being officially recognized."

"So, my son didn't die?" Tubby asked, stepping into the room beside Spikes, his expression a mix of hope and disbelief.

"He didn't. But his friend did. They intended to kill Dave to undermine monogamy. However, they ended up killing both him and his friend—or they thought they did. I found Dave, nursed him back to health, and raised him as my own. I renamed him Ramonito."

Gino glanced between Spikes and Tubby, confusion etched on his face. He realized only his father could have orchestrated such a plan. In a voice barely above a whisper, he said, "I will testify against my father."

China stood, moving to kiss Gino gently. "I want to assure you, Gino, that for as long as we both live, I am yours and you are mine. My love for you doesn't diminish my feelings for Dave. I choose to live with you, and I will always be faithful and loyal."

"The love we speak of transcends mere physicality," Ramonito added. "To Lovelyn, I say: you are very welcome to our family. I would be proud to see you and Leo raise your own family."

With renewed energy, they returned to the dining table. Surprisingly, China found herself quite hungry after the earlier chaos.

THREE DAYS AFTER

THE MONKEY AGE OF ENLIGHTENMENT

"From this day forward, and for all capuchin monkeys in this park, I declare that promiscuity is strictly forbidden!" Tubby proclaimed in his booming voice. The surrounding monkeys shook their branches in approval, celebrating the new law of their land (or trees).

The next day, Haig was expelled from the park and sent to the zoo, where he eventually met his demise at the jaws of a boa constrictor.

A week later, Lovelyn and Leo wed in what was celebrated as the wedding of the century.

Spikes and Tubby led their troops into an era that many monkey historians would later refer to as the Age of Enlightenment.

However, this period was later challenged when a young monkey boldly insisted that monkeys did not descend from humans. Historians remain divided on whether his name was Darren, Darlene, or Darwin.

And so it was.

THE SEARCH

"It's right beside you, sir."

Ed blinked, his gaze shifting from the dining table to the side table beside his chair. "Oh! Sorry, I was just admiring the... coffee." He sheepishly picked up the cup, only to discover a small feast waiting for him.

"I thought you'd like mangga, puto, and sikwate, sir," the helper said, a knowing smile on his face. The aroma of sticky rice and rich chocolate drink wafted through the air, transporting Ed back to his childhood days when his mother would whip up this breakfast masterpiece. It had to be over forty years since he'd indulged in this delightful combination.

"In Pinamungajan, breakfast isn't complete without them!"

Ed chuckled softly, memories flooding back. He remembered his father's stories about this town, tales that ignited a longing to return. After his father's passing two years ago, Ed felt a pull to retrace their roots, hoping that the mountains and rivers of Pinamungajan would help him complete his thesis on geodetic engineering.

As he took a sip, he mused, "Who knew coffee could come with a side of nostalgia?"

"Sir, your tour guide is here," the helper announced, stepping aside for Filemon to enter.

"Good morning, Sir!" Filemon bowed his stocky frame, exuding strength. His handshake was solid yet friendly.

"Morning! So, how long is our trip today? And, uh, should I be worried?" Ed asked, trying to keep the nerves at bay.

"It'll be a long trek, sir! Quite the adventure! But don't worry, everything will be alright in the end. If it's not alright, it's not the end!" Filemon grinned, his confidence infectious.

The morning sun cast long shadows as Ed and Filemon set off on their adventure. Ed, laden with a backpack full of anticipation, contrasted sharply with Filemon, who carried nothing but the weight of countless tours.

"We'll reach our first stop in about three hours, sir," Filemon said, his words as familiar as the trail beneath their feet. He'd guided hundreds, maybe thousands, through this landscape. His confidence was a comforting presence, born from years of navigating the hidden treasures of Pinamungajan—caves, waterfalls, and secrets whispered on the wind. He'd traded his unfinished civil engineering degree for the stories of this land, a trade made necessary when his mother fell ill, a trade that had lasted until her death three years ago.

Filemon was a walking encyclopedia, comfortable discussing everything from philosophy to theology. He could charm the birds from the trees with his words, except when it came to one topic...

They walked in comfortable silence for a while, their footsteps a steady beat against the morning quiet. Then, Ed, emboldened by the peaceful atmosphere, decided to break the silence.

"Filemon," Ed began, "Is your family... still here?"

Filemon paused, the question hanging in the air like a silent prayer. Ed immediately regretted his intrusion. "Oh, I'm sorry. Don't answer if you don't want to," he mumbled, feeling his cheeks flush.

Filemon sighed, a hint of weariness in his voice. "It's alright. My mother... she passed away three years ago. A long, painful illness. It was hard on both of us, you know? The living and the dead."

A shared silence fell between them, heavy with unspoken grief. Then, as if drawn by an unseen force, they both stopped and turned towards the house. As Ed stepped out, he gasped. The rising sun painted the church bell towers a vibrant orange, a breathtaking sight that instantly brightened his mood.

"Filemon," Ed said, a newfound energy in his voice, "Let's stop by the church first." He started walking, leaving Filemon to catch up, a smile playing on his lips. The unexpected detour felt right, a moment of peace before the adventure truly began.

The air hung crisp and cool, heavy with the scent of damp earth and the lingering perfume of rain. Dew clung to the grass like tiny diamonds. Inside the church, the silence was thick enough to cut with a knife. Ed and Filemon knelt in the back pews, their prayers a silent communion with the ancient stones.

After a few moments, Ed rose abruptly, his gaze fixed on the choir loft and the rickety wooden stairs leading to the abandoned bell tower. Filemon watched, a mixture of apprehension and curiosity etched on his face.

"Whatever you're thinking, sir," Filemon muttered, "I'm not climbing that *kampanaryo*." He gestured towards the dilapidated stairs, some of which were replaced with precarious-looking bamboo. "It looks like it's about to collapse—along with me!"

Ed's eyes, however, remained glued to the stairs. "Can you help me get up there?" he asked, his voice firm despite the inherent danger.

Filemon's eyes widened. "Oh no, no, no! That's not in the itinerary, sir! Whatever you're looking for is *definitely* not up there. Absolutely not. Certainly not!" He was visibly trembling.

Ed sighed, understanding Filemon's apprehension. "Okay, let's move on then."

Filemon, already halfway to the church exit, practically sprinted out the door. The silence that followed was deafening, broken only by the chirping of crickets.

Finally, Filemon cleared his throat. "Sir...may I ask what your thesis is about?"

Ed, still gazing longingly at the bell tower, chuckled slightly. "Well, I'm studying geodetic engineering. I'm hoping to find something here in Pinamungajan that I can use in my theory on surveying, mapping, remote sensing, GIS... the works."

"And do you plan to use your findings to improve this town, the country, or somewhere else?" Filemon pressed, his tone thoughtful.

Ed hesitated. He wasn't sure how to answer.

"I've lived here my whole life," Filemon began, his voice low and contemplative, "and I see friends, relatives, classmates... they all go abroad, send money back. But is that really enough?" He paused, his gaze distant. "There's got to be more to it than just money, right?"

Ed was intrigued. "You're right," he said. "Sending money helps, of course. The Asian financial crisis in '97 is a good example. The remittances from OFWs really helped the Philippines recover."

"Exactly!" Filemon exclaimed. "But there's more to progress than just money. It's about... well, it's complicated."

"Filemon," Ed interrupted, a smile playing on his lips, "Please, call me Ed. Edgardo is a bit much."

"Sure, Sir Ed... I mean, Ed... sir... Ed," Filemon stammered, breaking into laughter.

"As soon as we cross this river," Ed said, his eyes fixed on the slippery rocks ahead, "we can continue this discussion. For now... focus!" He carefully picked his way across the rocks, muttering, "Oops...oops..." The clear water, the vibrant green plants—they were a refreshing distraction from his academic musings.

Three hours melted away like morning dew. Ed, his muscles protesting, was ready to collapse when he rounded a bend and gasped. Before him, nestled in a valley cradled by towering limestone cliffs, lay a sight that stole his breath—a seemingly endless expanse of turquoise water, shimmering under the deep blue sky. For a moment, he thought he'd stumbled onto a hidden ocean, perched high in the mountains.

Filemon, ever the showman, beamed. "That, my friend, is the Hidden Valley Mountain Resort! Our first stop." He waved his hand with the flourish of a seasoned maestro presenting his masterpiece. "And the main attraction? The wave pool! The first of its kind in all of Cebu!" He nudged Ed forward, a mischievous glint in his eye.

A wave of pride washed over Ed. This was *his* hometown, a place of unexpected beauty.

They found a table at the resort's coffee shop, overlooking the wave pool. The aroma of freshly brewed coffee filled the air. "Oregano coffee," Filemon announced, "My personal favorite." Ed took a sip, the unique flavor a delightful surprise.

While Ed furiously typed notes on his iPad, snapping photos and selfies, Filemon watched him with a knowing smile. The quiet was broken only by the click-clack of the keyboard and the gentle lapping of waves. Then, Filemon leaned in, his eyes intense.

"Ed," he said, "look around you. What's your best contribution to *this*?"

Ed froze. He'd been so focused on his research, he hadn't considered the bigger picture. He knew, from their earlier conversation, that money wasn't the answer Filemon was looking for.

After a long pause, Ed finally spoke. "I don't want to be a product of my environment," he said thoughtfully. "I want the environment to be a product of *me*."

Filemon's smile widened. "Excellent. Now, let's see the rest of what Pinamungajan has to offer before we discuss how you can give back to your hometown."

He launched into tour-guide mode, his voice brimming with enthusiasm. "Pinamungajan is a caver's paradise! One hundred and eighteen caves, and over one hundred of them are right here in this village. You'll find stunning stalactites and stalagmites..."

"Crawling?" Ed asked, a playful smirk on his face.

Filemon chuckled. "Ah, your Cebuano is still sharp! 'Kamangon'—it comes from 'kamang,' meaning 'to crawl.' You'll have to crawl a bit to get into the Kamangon Cave, but it's worth it. After that, we're off to the Twin Falls. It's a short walk, but... a bit challenging."

"Safe?" Ed asked, a hint of apprehension in his voice. "Are we going to be alright?"

Filemon winked. "Remember what I said? It'll be alright in the end. If it's not alright, it's not the end." They both laughed, the tension easing.

The caves were breathtaking. Ed marvelled at the intricate formations, his geodetic mind momentarily forgetting gravitational fields and crustal motion. He found himself transported back to his childhood, imagining the villagers who had sought shelter within these ancient stones during the war. The Twin Falls were even more magnificent, a double cascade of water tumbling into a crystal-clear pool. The sheer power and beauty of nature overwhelmed him.

Their journey continued to Liki Falls, another stunning waterfall hidden amidst lush greenery. Filemon, with a mischievous grin, refused to translate the name, leaving Ed to wonder at its meaning. The sight of people swimming in the cool water was tempting, but Ed, ever the cautious academic, decided against a spontaneous dip.

The sound of rushing water, the rustling leaves, the earthy scent of the forest—it was all utterly captivating. Ed, lost in the moment, forgot his surroundings. Then, with a startled yelp, he lost his footing. A slippery rock sent him tumbling down the muddy bank, with a resounding "Aaaaarrrrrgh!" and a big splash.

Filemon was instantly at his side, pulling him from the water. Other swimmers rushed to help, hauling Ed onto the grassy bank.

"I think I broke my leg!" Ed groaned, clutching his ankle.

A young man pushed his way through the crowd. "Please, let me through! My uncle's a doctor." He expertly examined Ed's leg, removing his shoe and pulling up his pants. A trickle of blood appeared below his knee. After a quick assessment, he declared, "No broken bones, just some nasty bruises. Your ankle's going to swell, but you'll be alright." He turned to Filemon. "Get him to your place. Rest it, and we'll check on him later."

Filemon's house was simple but welcoming, overlooking a vast rice paddy. Lunch was a feast, a far cry from the usual fare Ed was accustomed to. The house was impeccably clean, yet it felt lived-in, comfortable. After the meal, Filemon helped Ed to a chair, propping his injured leg on a small wooden box.

Ed's eyes were drawn to an old cabinet, its surface adorned with photos, trophies, and medals. In the center, a large image of Mary, Mother of Perpetual Help, dominated a mirror. But it was a small photo tucked in the corner that caught his attention—a faded picture of a beautiful woman cradling two babies, about a year old, clearly twins. The right side of the photo was torn. Ed stared, mesmerized. A wave of dizziness washed over him; his legs felt like jelly. He swayed, about to fall, when Filemon caught him, gently guiding him back to the chair near the window.

The sun was still high in the sky, casting a warm glow over the landscape. Filemon decided they would rest for an hour. He glanced at Ed, who sat with his eyes closed, deep in thought. But something seemed off—Ed's arms were shaking. Filemon leaned in, his heart racing. Was Ed... crying?

"Filemon," Ed whispered, barely audible, "you asked what I can offer to our town. I don't think I have a straight answer." His voice quivered, thick with emotion.

"Oh my God, you don't have to shake and cry over that!" Filemon exclaimed, half-excited, half-concerned. "It's just a question!"

Ed managed a weak smile, wiping his eyes. "I'm not quite sure how to explain it."

"By the way," Filemon interjected, eager to shift the mood, "I know the perfect place to discuss that topic. Let's head to Campalabo Sandbar!"

He continued, his enthusiasm infectious. "It's a beautiful strip of white sand, just twenty minutes from here. During low tide, it spans about a hectare, but it gets smaller when the tide comes in. It's rich in marine life and offers a stunning view of the coastline. Plus, it's right by a marine sanctuary, perfect for snorkeling! Though... I'm not sure how up for that you are." He winked, a teasing smile on his face.

"From Campalabo, we can head to one of the beach resorts in Tajao and catch the sunset," he added, laying out the next leg of their journey.

Ed couldn't help but grin at Filemon's enthusiasm. As they made their way back into town, the serene plaza in front of the Municipal Hall greeted them, and a flood of childhood memories rushed back—jumping from the dike during high tide, building elaborate sand structures during low tide. His favorite was a race track with winding curves, just big enough for his slippers to navigate. The dike looked cleaner now, free of plastic and clutter, smelling fresh and inviting.

They boarded one of the boats waiting on the shore, the motor roaring to life beneath them. As they sped towards Campalabo, the wind tousled Ed's hair, and he felt a sense of freedom. Amidst the roar of the engine, Filemon turned to him and asked, "You've seen so much of Pinamungajan. Is your life abroad really that much better?"

"In some ways, yes," Ed replied, the words flowing more easily now. "There's less pollution, for one. You don't see garbage and traffic? Well, even when it exists, drivers actually stay in their lanes! Parks and gardens are plentiful, well-maintained, and they're free."

Filemon nodded, intrigued. "So what can you offer back to your town?"

Ed paused, considering his words carefully. "So many ideas and concepts from abroad could work here. With the right mindset, things can really change. People who have traveled overseas often have great ideas to share. I definitely do."

Before he could elaborate further, the boatman shouted, "Here we are, sir! Campalabo Sandbar!"

Ed stood mesmerized by the clear waters of Campalabo Sandbar, gazing at the small islet before him. "No trees on this island? Does it all disappear underwater during high tide?" he wondered aloud, taking in the breathtaking view of the Pinamungajan coastline stretching to the east.

With the sun at his back, the full beauty of the town unfolded before him—a sight that had once existed only in his memories. Time felt endless as he and Filemon enjoyed the warm water, swimming and chatting about the future of Pinamungajan.

Amidst their playful banter, Ed caught himself glancing at Filemon, unsure if it was before or after he'd removed his shirt. The sun was setting, casting a golden hue over everything, and their conversation shifted to the town's progress and how they could contribute to it.

But as the sky darkened, it was time to leave Campalabo. They hopped back into the boat, the engine roaring to life as they sped toward the beach resorts of Tajao. There, they were greeted by a woman whose features were strikingly familiar.

"Wait a minute, is she your twin sister?" Ed blurted out, pointing at Filemon.

"Yes, she is! This is Jane, the manager of the beach resort. Jane, meet Ed."

"Nice to meet you, Ed," Jane said with a warm smile.

"My pleasure, Jane! Are you the other baby in that picture?" Ed asked with curiosity.

"What picture?" Jane replied, tilting her head.

Ed glanced at Filemon. "When we were at your house, I saw a photo of a woman holding two babies."

"Ah, yes! That picture!" Jane and Filemon chorused, their voices harmonizing like all twins do, and they both smiled.

Ed pulled out a small photo from his wallet, and the twins' expressions shifted. "I've been carrying this since Papa gave it to me two years ago," he said, revealing a faded image of a man holding a six-year-old boy, the left side torn.

All three exchanged charged glances.

"Is that why you kept looking at me after we left my house? Oh my God, I thought for a moment that you were gay or something!" Filemon teased, a playful grin spreading across his face.

Ed chuckled nervously. "I came here searching for something for my thesis, and instead, I found my siblings. Papa made me promise to find the other half of this photo. He would be so happy to know you're alright."

"A man travels the world over in search of what he needs and returns home to find it," Filemon said, his smile warm and knowing.

"Indeed. Just like our town. People go to all these other places, even abroad, looking for better lives, only to realize there's so much beauty right in their own backyard," Jane added softly.

Ed's voice cracked, a tear rolling down his cheek. "Now I know I'm right where I belong."

"Welcome home, Manoy Ed," Jane whispered, her own eyes glistening with tears.

In an emotional embrace, the siblings cried, releasing years of pent-up feelings. Like a volcano, they erupted in joy, finding the lost pieces of their lives in the hometown where it all began.

Outside, the sunset painted the sky in hues of orange and pink, reflecting the joy of their reunion as they let the past fade into the night, eagerly awaiting a new dawn filled with hope and possibilities.

THE END

Danny Ninal has a Bachelor's Degree in Philosophy and English
from San Carlos Seminary College, Cebu City, Philippines.
His interests include Christian History, Philosophy, Law,
Systematic Theology, Classical and Modern Literature,
Poetry, Economics, Politics, Business Management,
Information Technology Systems, and Music.
All these converge into one potent writing machine
which puts into the written word a juxta-position
of profound messages beautifully intertwined
with compelling storylines.
Danny is currently the Lead Pastor
of World Harvest Fellowship – Auckland.
He lives in Auckland City, New Zealand,
with his wife, Jia, and his only daughter, Danielle Angelika.

Previous books published by Danny Niñal
    Charity Is Missing
    Siblings: The Brothers of Mercy
    More Than Words, A Bible Study Guide for New Believers,
        Volumes 1 & 2
    Following Christ, A Journey of Faith

Short Stories written by Danny Niñal
    I Died Therefore I Am
    Appearances
    Flowers and the Bees
    What is Pleasure Without Pain
    The Search
    Love: A Monkey's Business
    I Luh Yah Pippa
    I Remember Papa

Printed by Libri Plureos GmbH in Hamburg, Germany